DISCOVERING BORDEAUX FRANCE

The Pearl of Aquitaine Pictorial

PICTORIAL SEARIES

Presented by

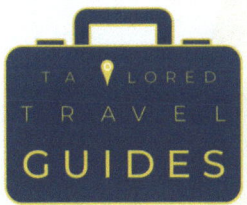

Discover your journey!

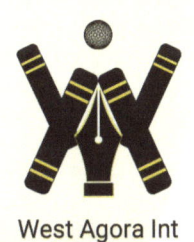

West Agora Int

a WEST AGORA INT S.R.L. Brand
www.tailoredtravelguides.com
Edited by WEST AGORA INT S.R.L.
WEST AGORA INT S.R.L. All Rights Reserved
Copyright © WEST AGORA INT S.R.L., 2023

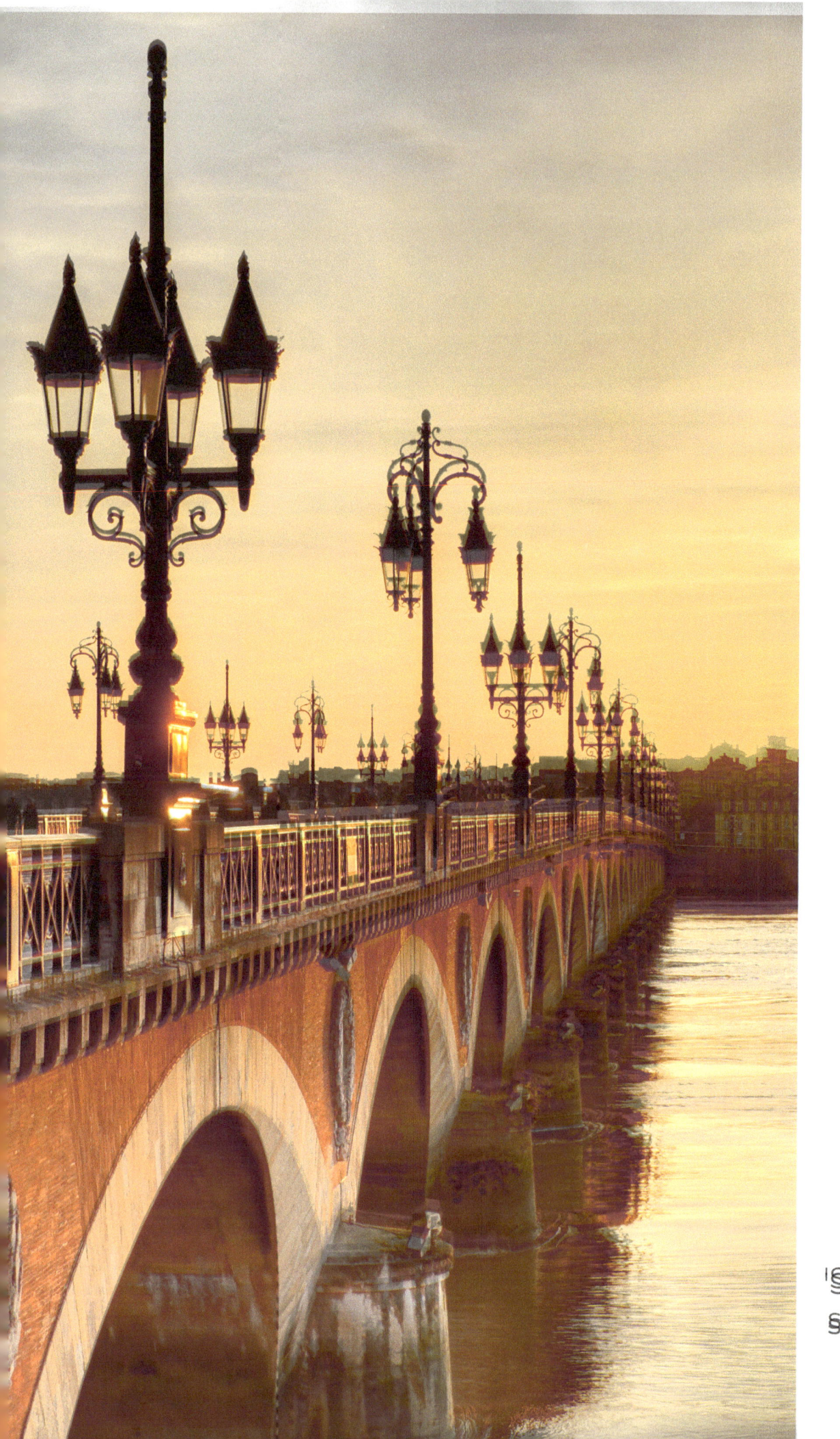

Pont de Pierre, or 'Stone Bridge' spanning the Garonne River

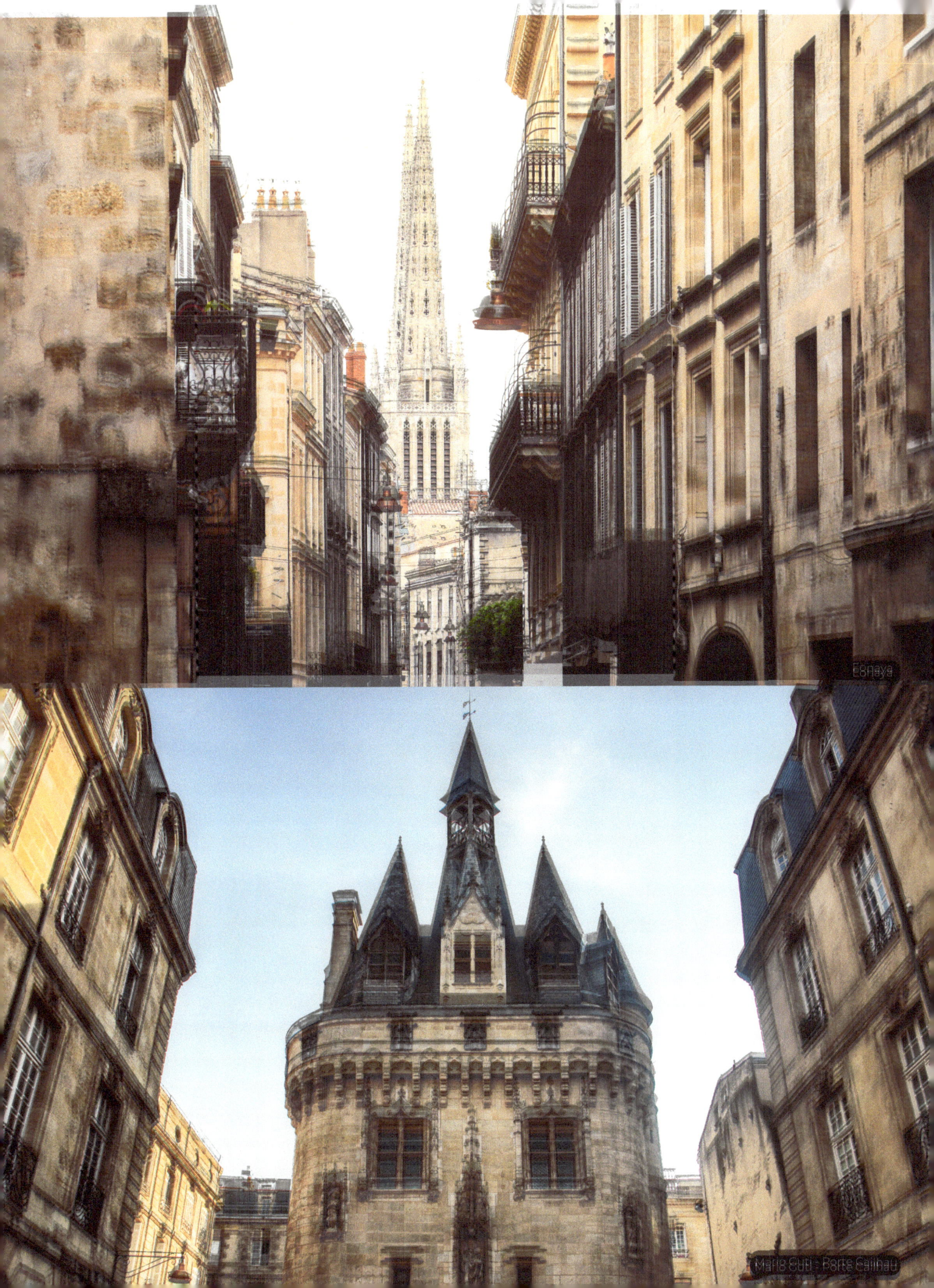

Place de la Bourse - designed in the 18th century by the famed architect Ange-Jacques Gabriel

Andrey Khrobostov

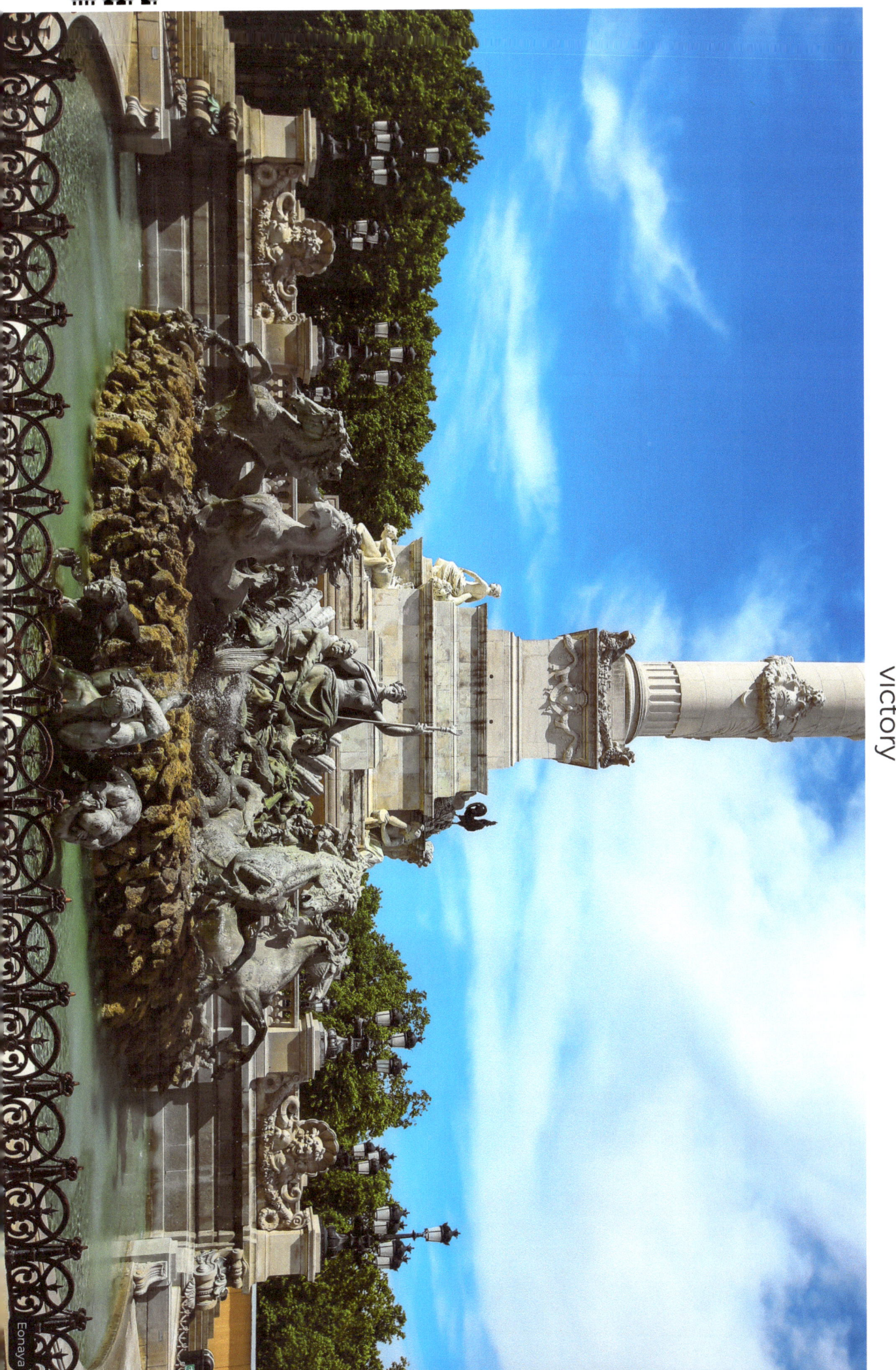

Ornate fountain and bronze sculptures in Place des Quinconces representing peace and victory

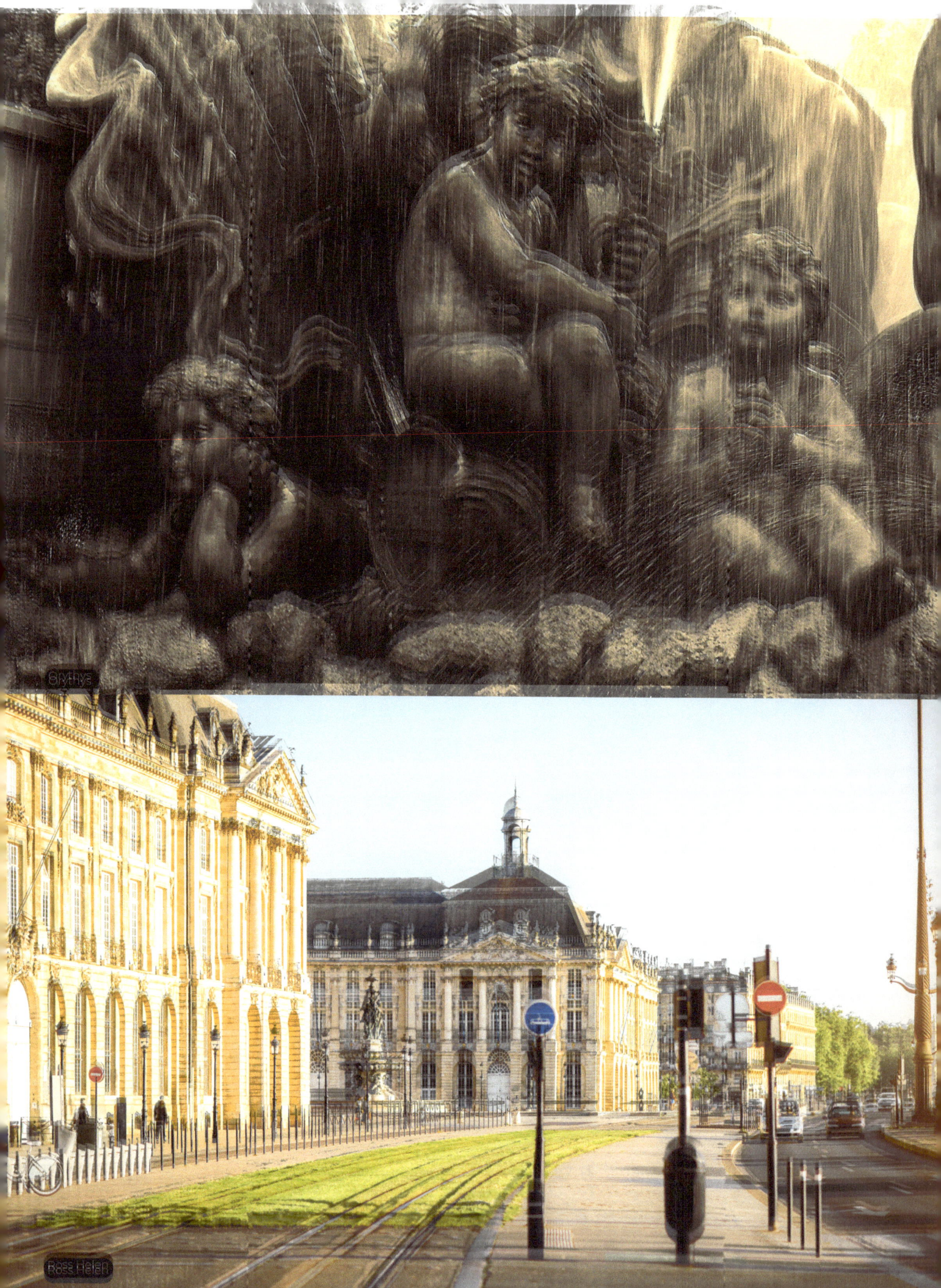

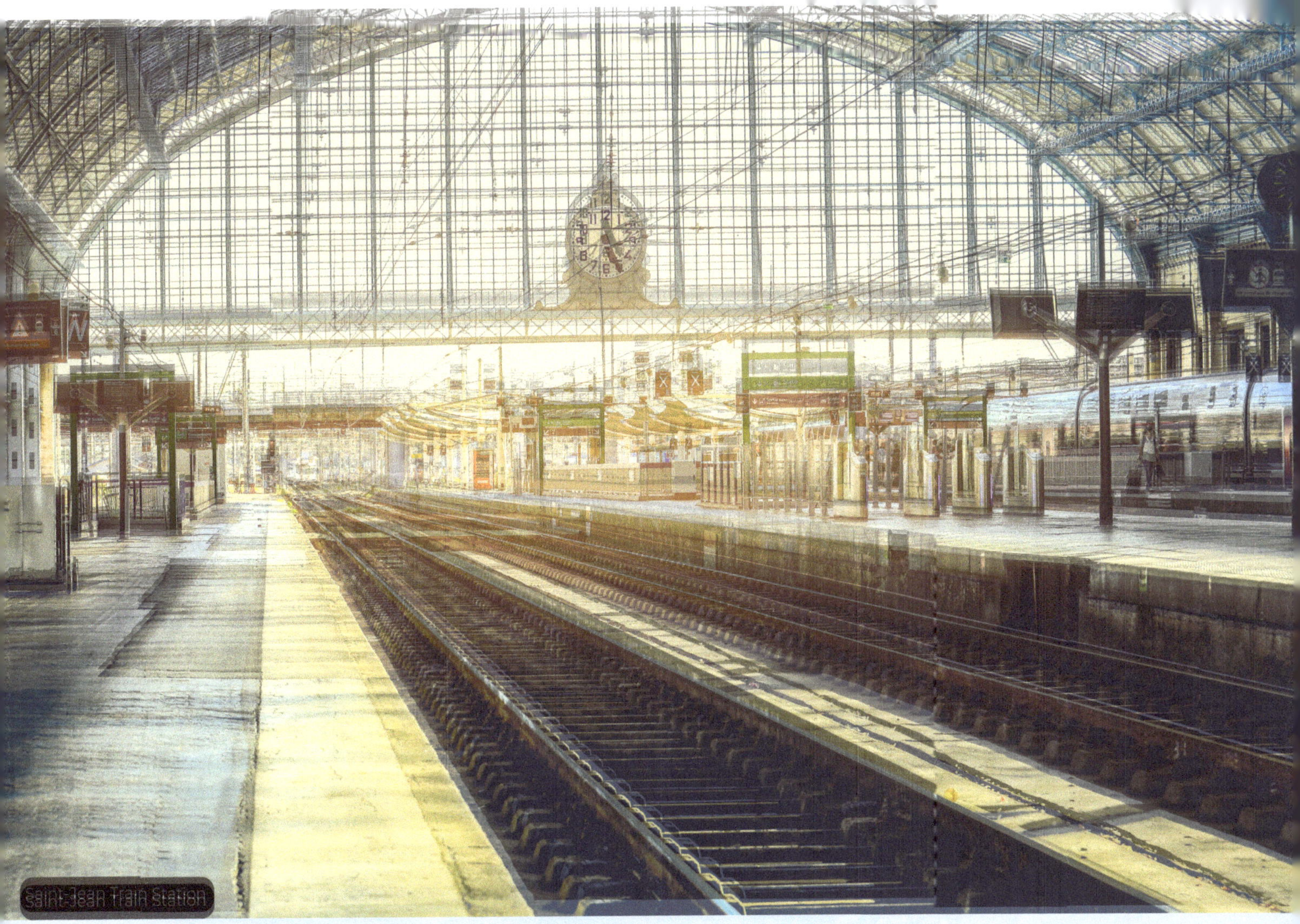

Saint-Jean Train Station

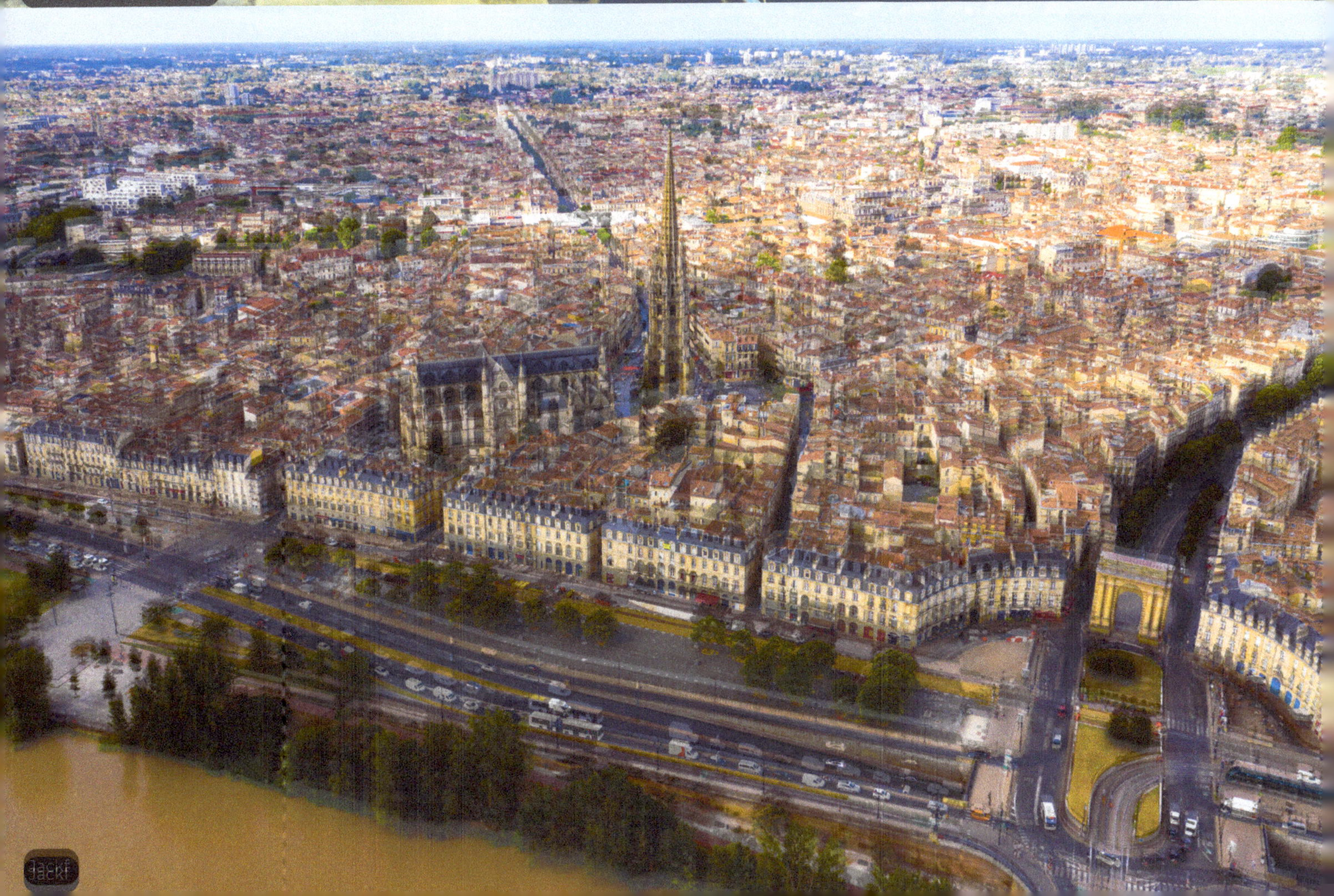

Bordeaux Cathedral

Nestled in the vibrant heart of Bordeaux, the Bordeaux Cathedral stands as a testament to the city's rich history and architectural prowess. Officially known as the Cathédrale Saint-André de Bordeaux, this Gothic masterpiece captivates visitors with its awe-inspiring façade and intricate stonework. Built over centuries, starting from the 12th century, the cathedral's eclectic mix of Romanesque and Gothic elements tells a story of architectural evolution. As you approach, the twin spires of the Pey-Berland tower command the skyline, offering a stunning contrast to the Bordeaux cityscape. The cathedral's exterior is adorned with sculptures and gargoyles, each telling tales from biblical and medieval times. The grandeur continues inside, where the vast nave creates a sense of celestial space. Stained glass windows bathe the interior in a kaleidoscope of colors, illuminating ancient frescoes and the intricately carved choir screen.

Not just a religious landmark, Bordeaux Cathedral has witnessed significant historical events, including the wedding of Eleanor of Aquitaine to the future Louis VII of France. This event forever linked Bordeaux to royal history and the broader narratives of Europe.

A visit to Bordeaux Cathedral is more than just a journey through history; it's an immersive experience in the timeless beauty of Gothic artistry, set in the world-renowned wine region of Aquitaine. Whether you're a history enthusiast or an admirer of architectural marvels, the Bordeaux Cathedral is a must-visit landmark in the Pearl of Aquitaine.

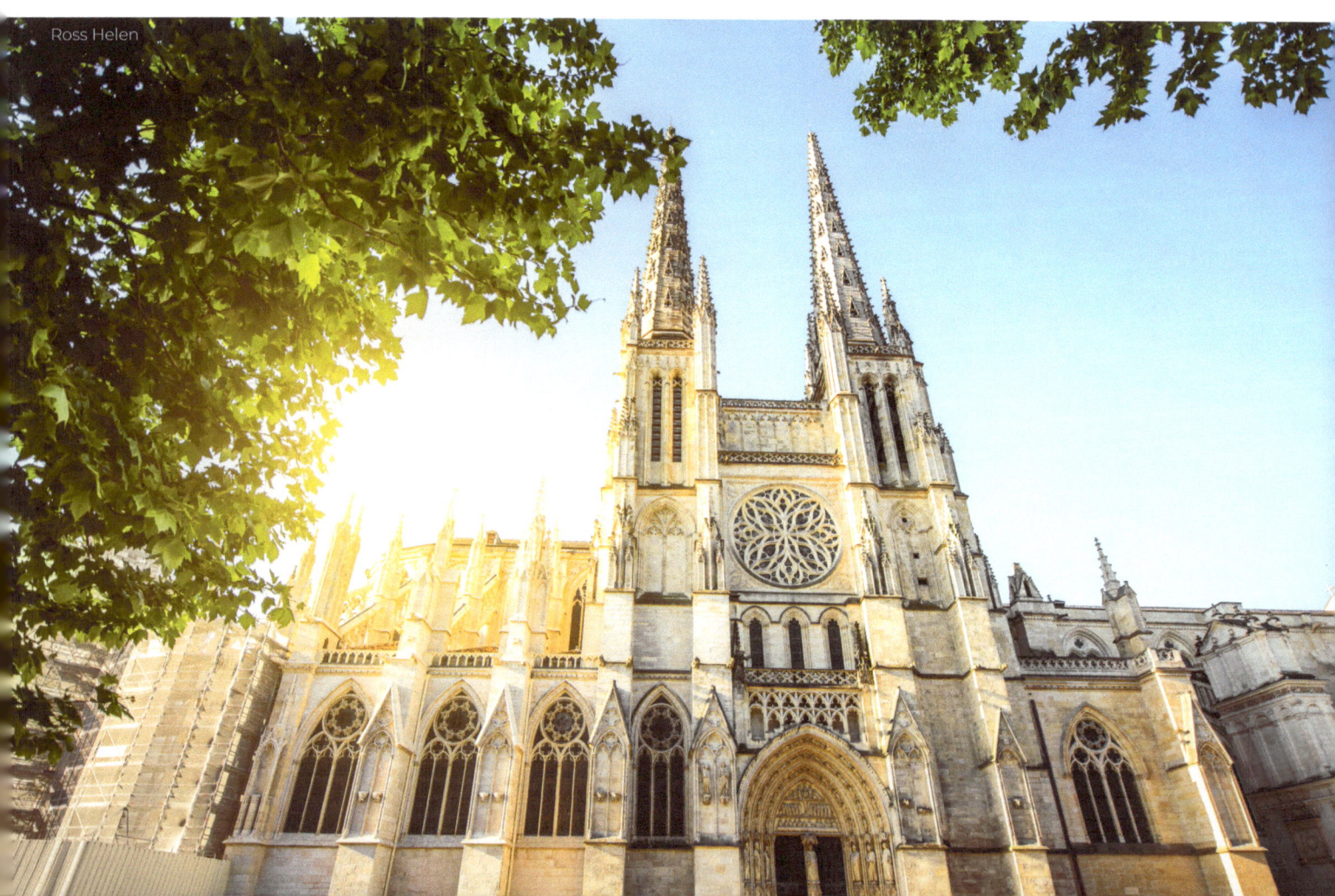
Ross Helen

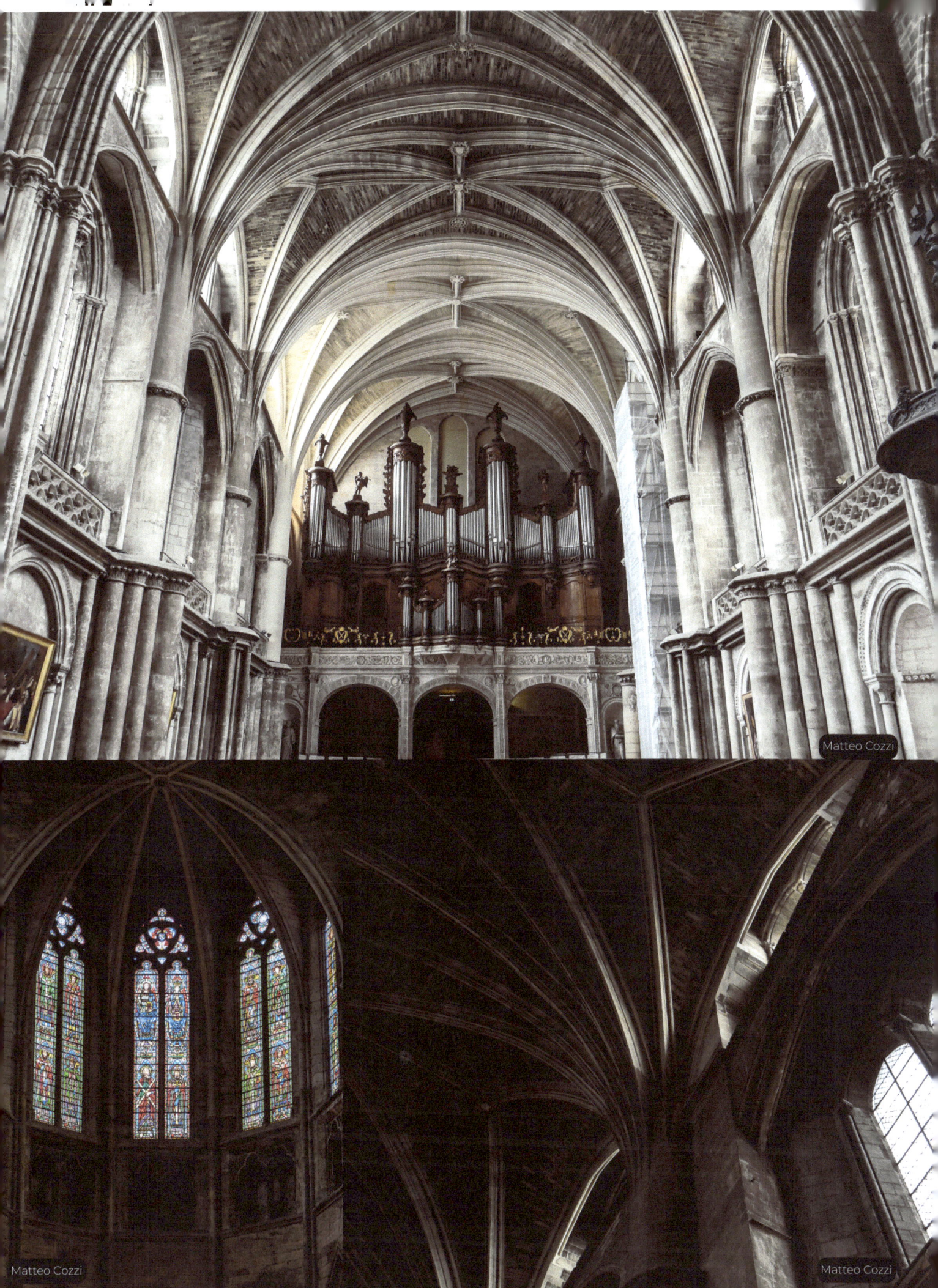

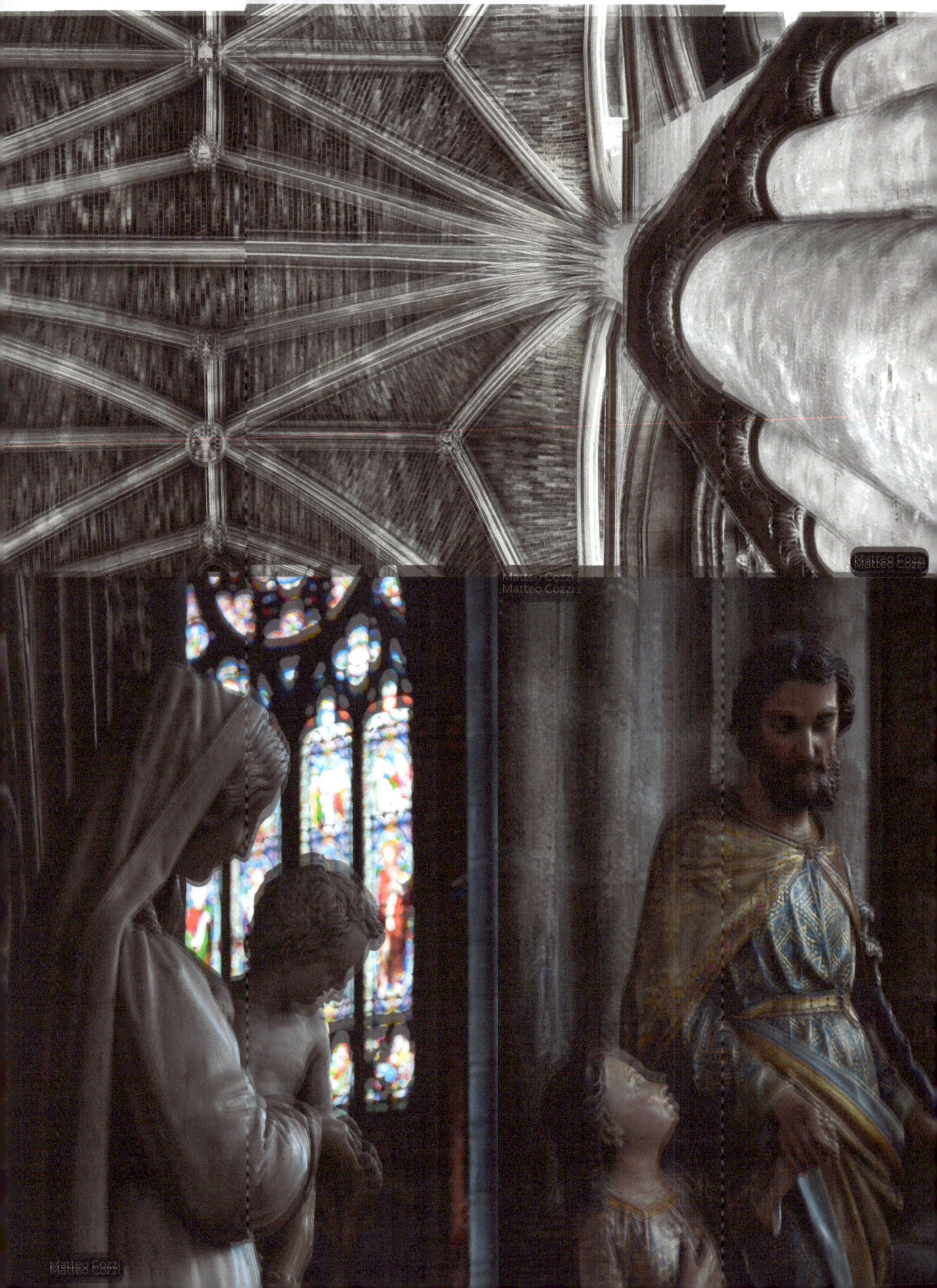

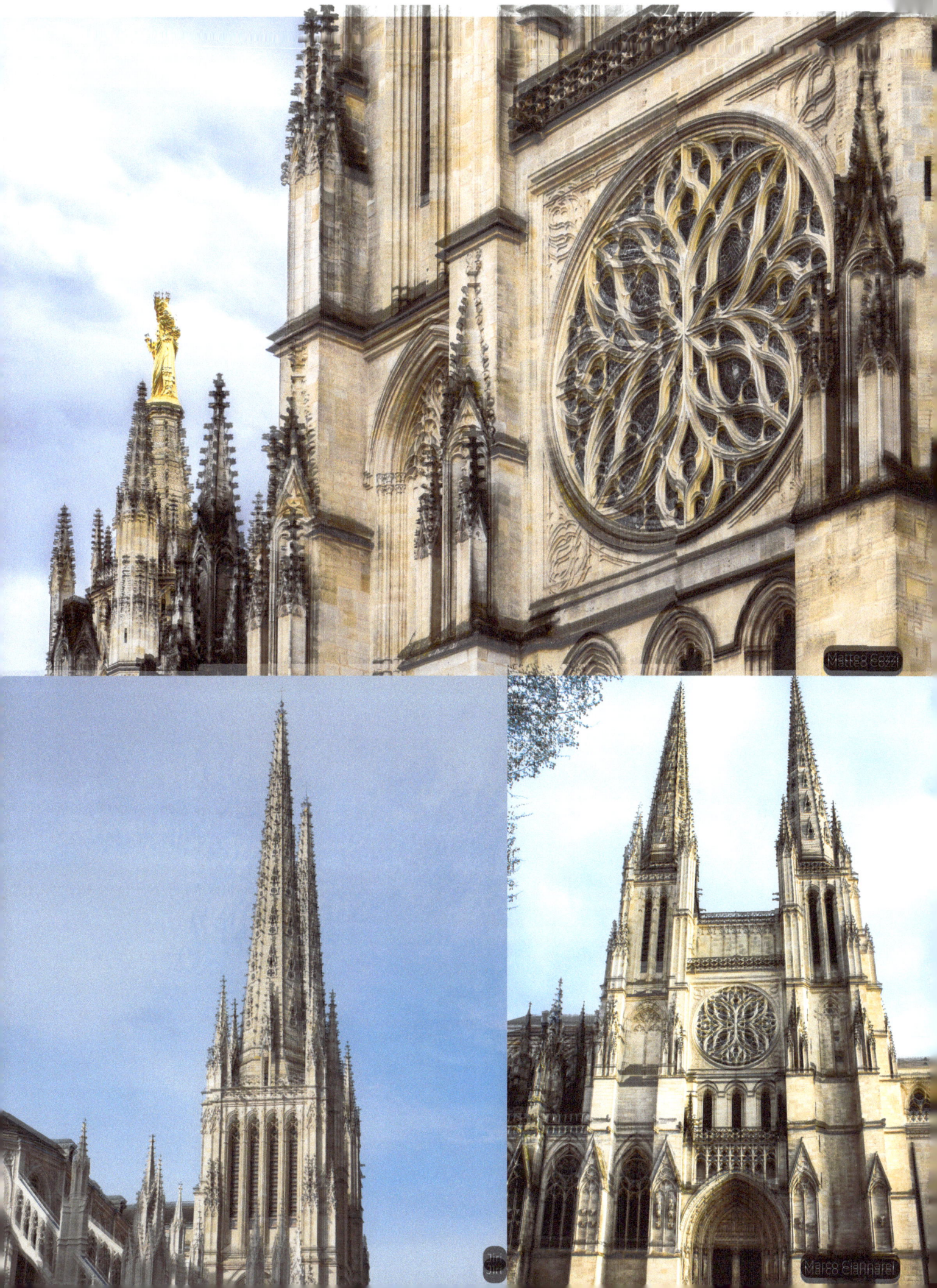

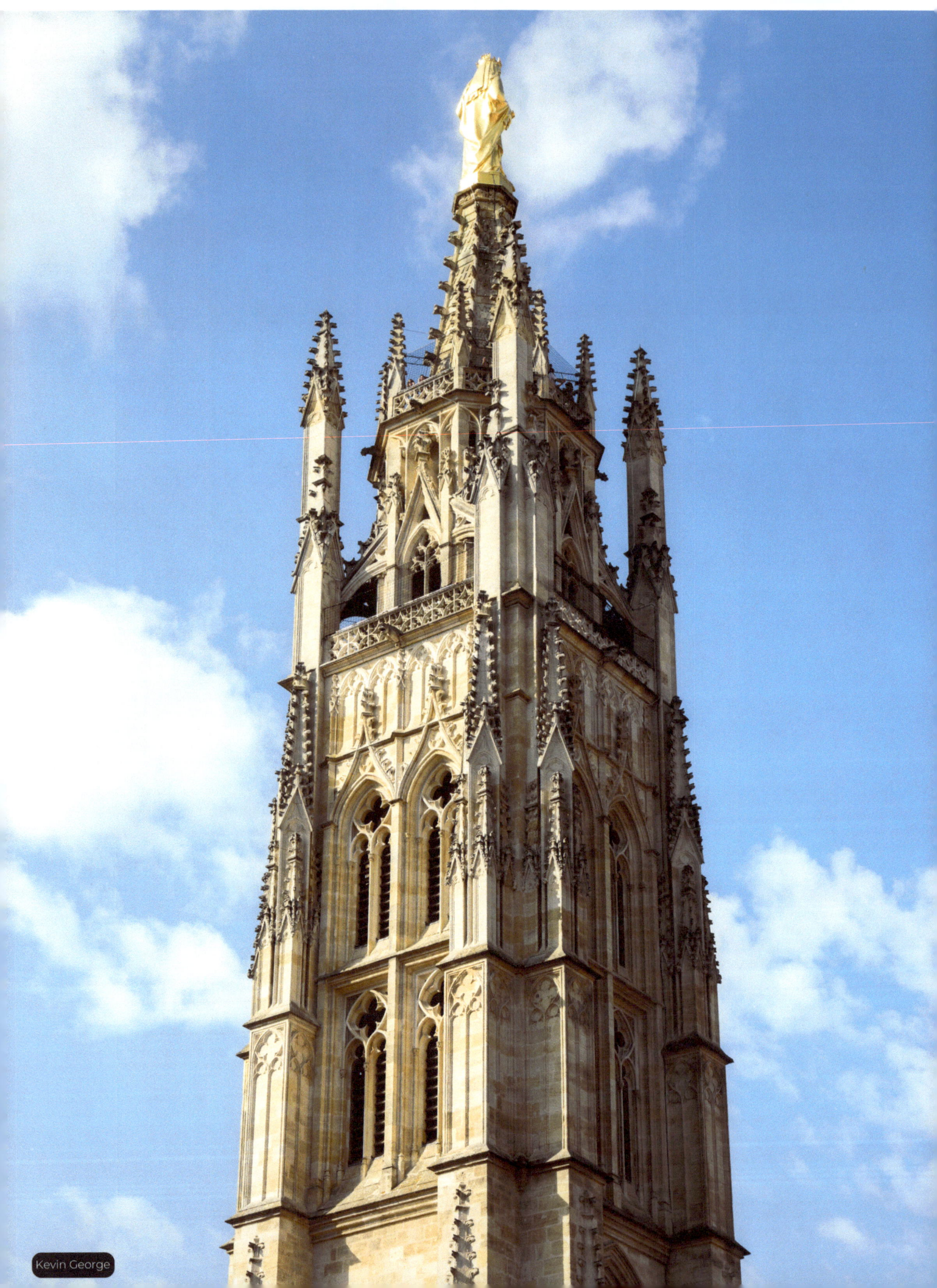

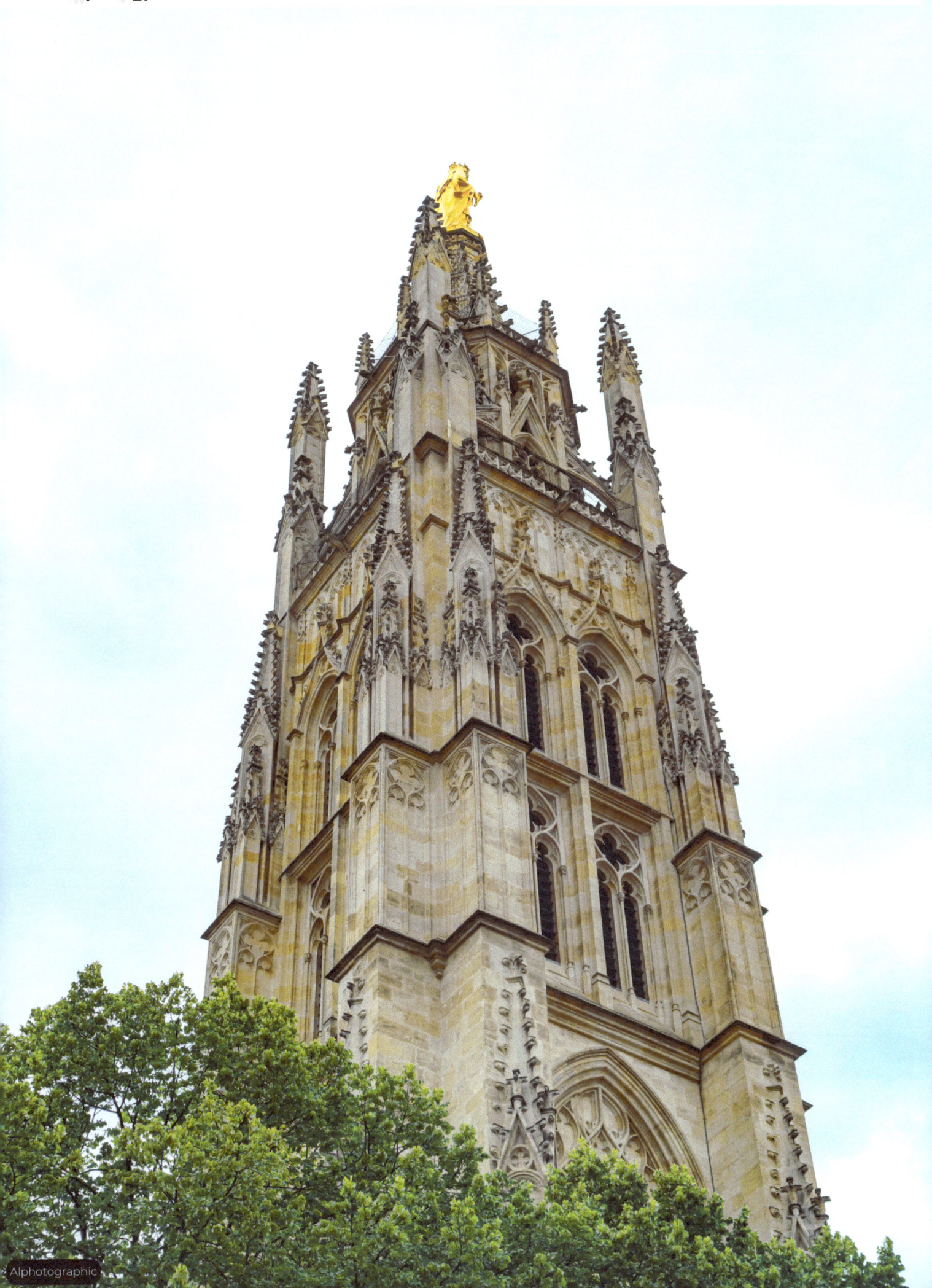

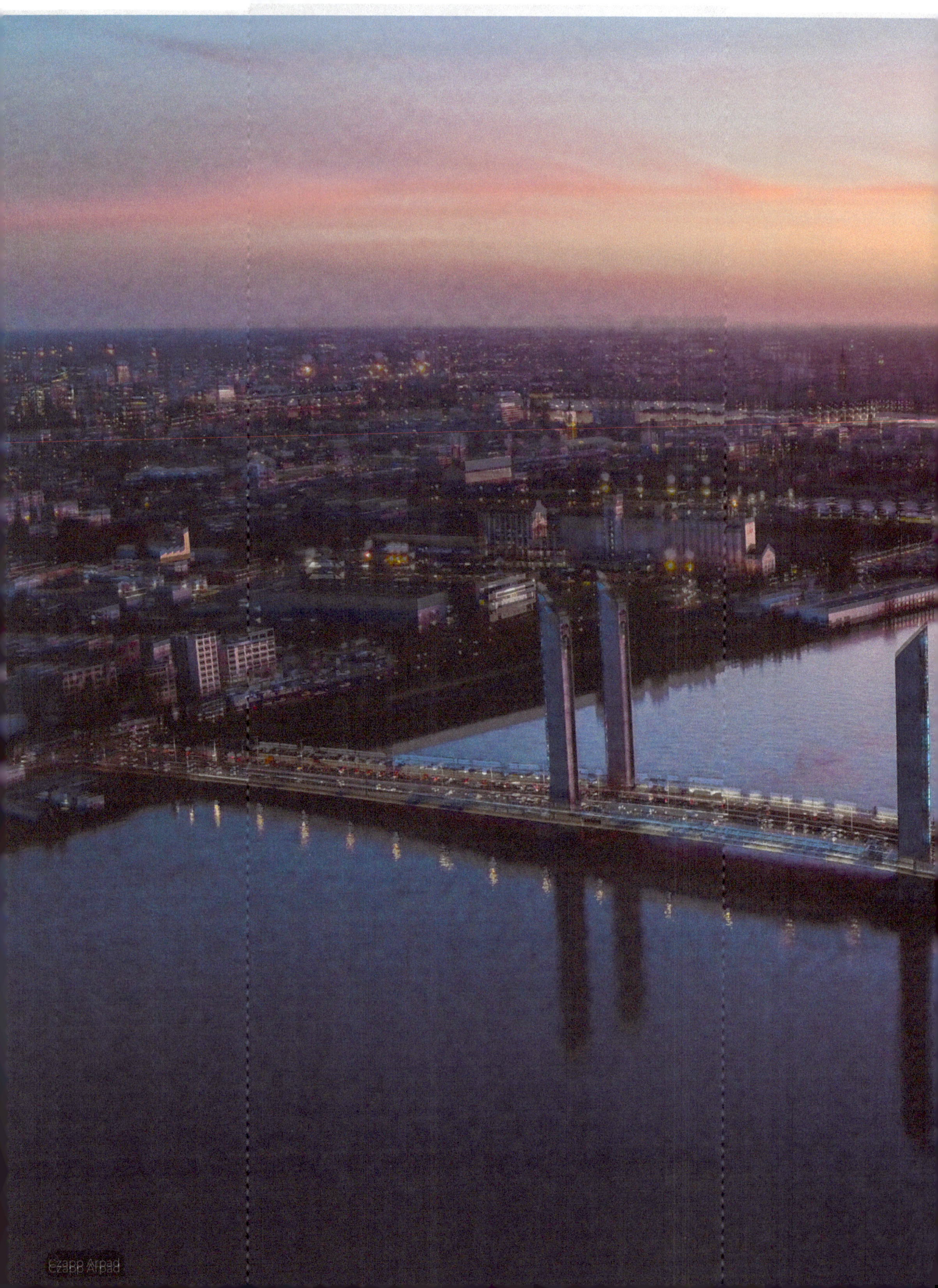

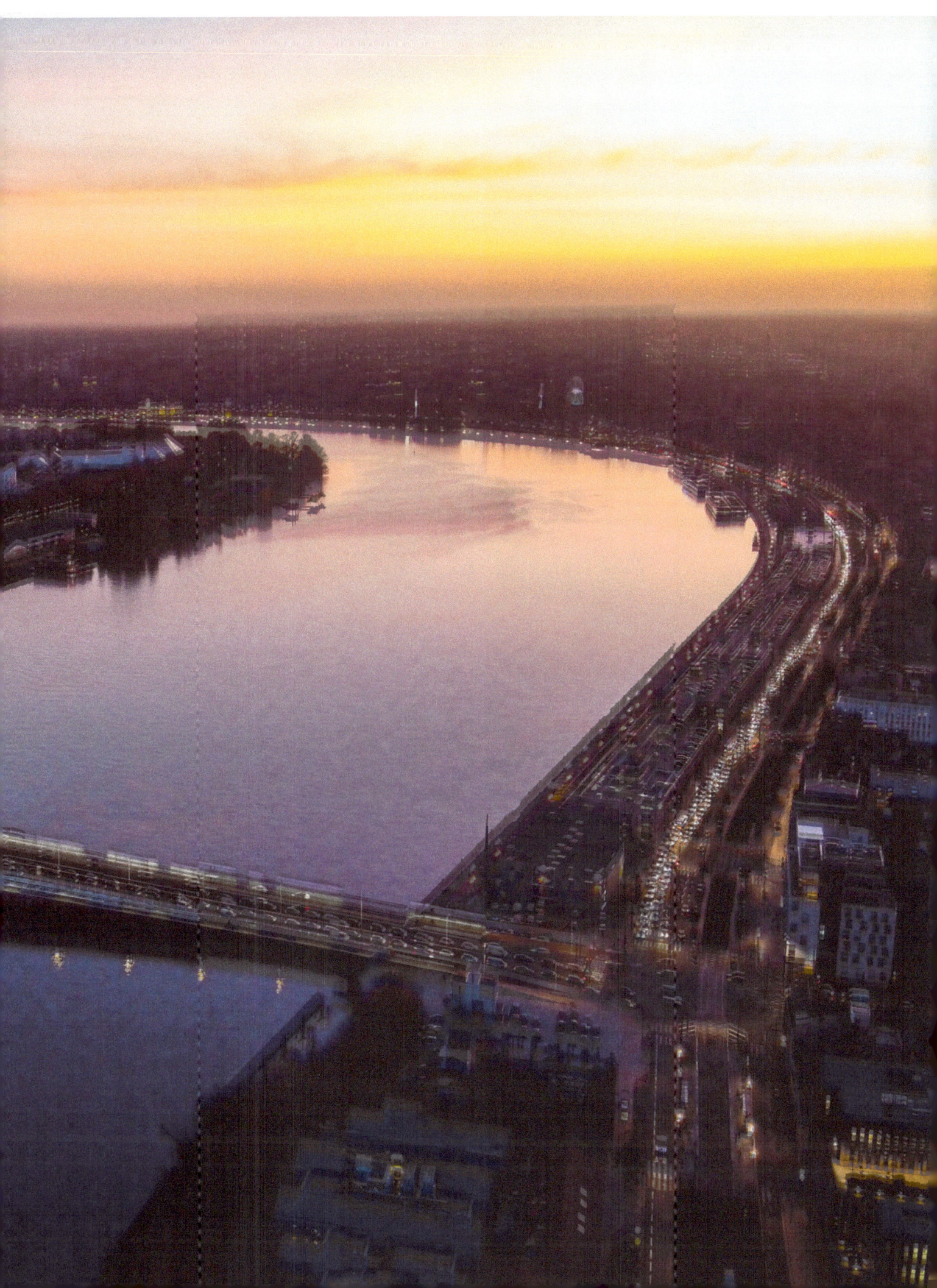

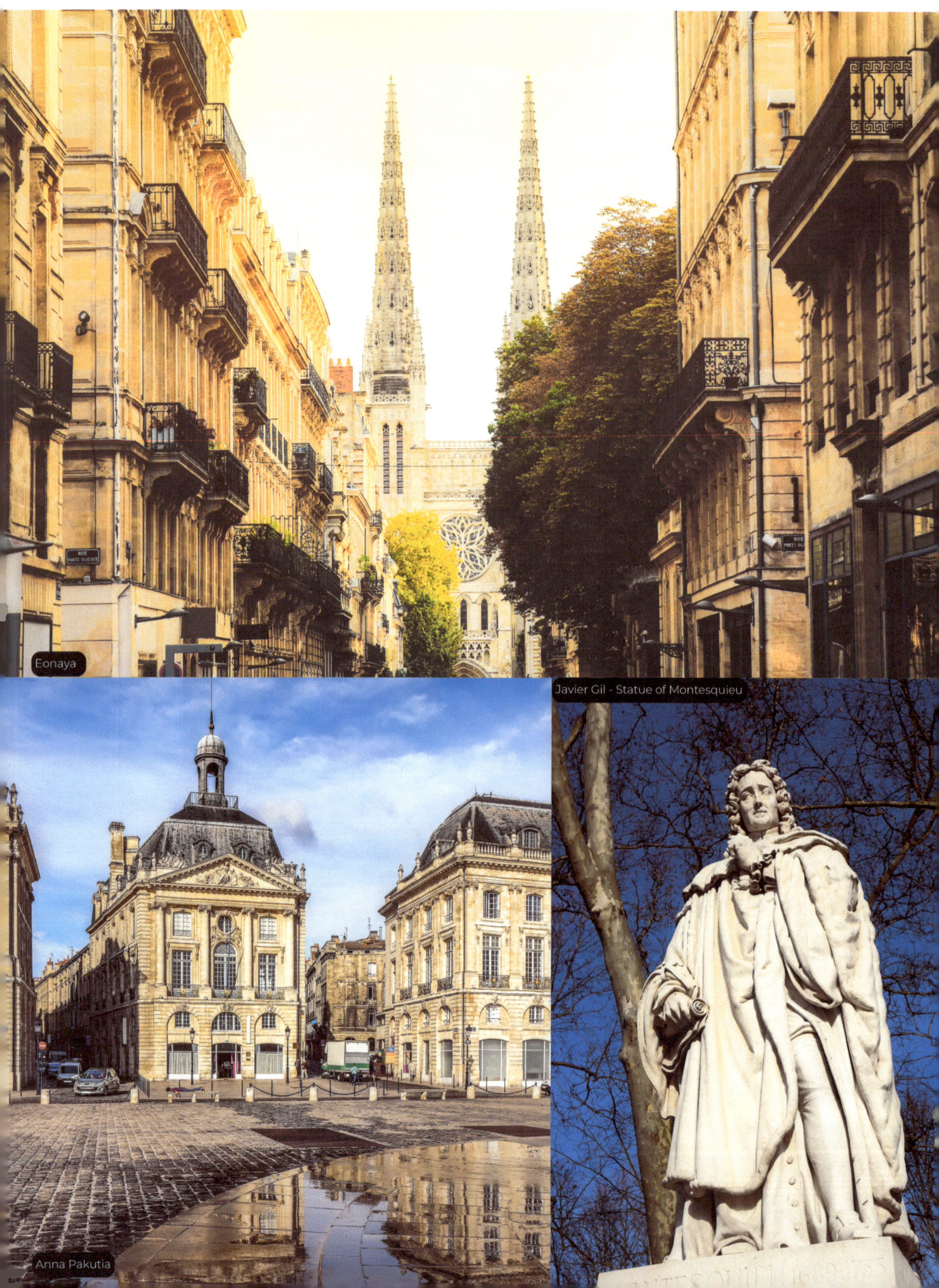

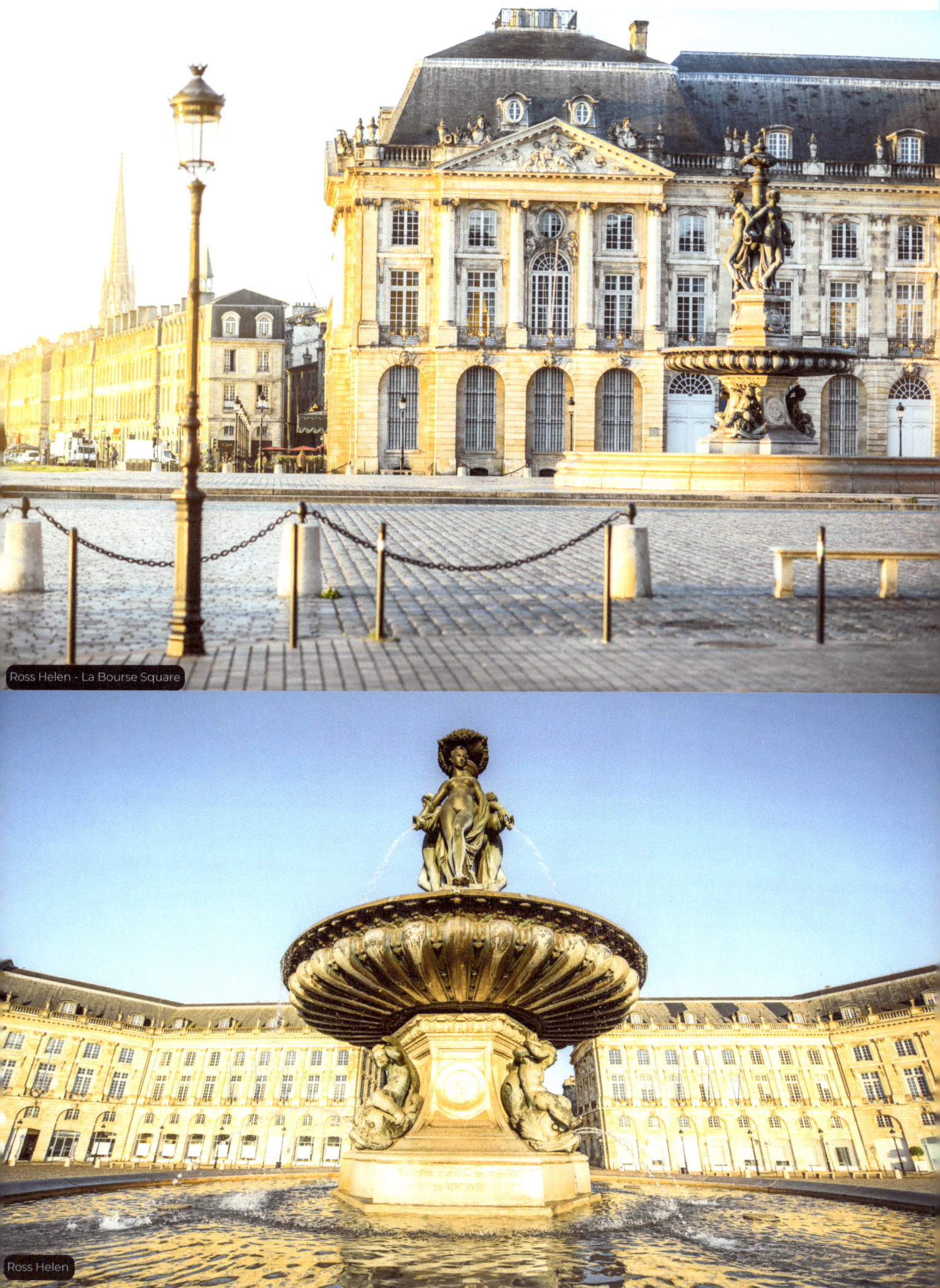

Ross Helen - La Bourse Square

Ross Helen

The Grosse Cloche

In the heart of Bordeaux's bustling city center stands The Grosse Cloche, an emblematic symbol of the city's medieval heritage. Known as the 'Great Bell', this historic monument dates back to the 15th century, serving as a vivid reminder of Bordeaux's rich past. The Grosse Cloche, with its two 40-meter-high circular towers and central bell, was once part of the old town hall and served as a gateway to the city. The bell itself, weighing an impressive 7,800 kilograms, has a story of its own. Traditionally rung during major events and celebrations, it has echoed through the ages, marking moments of significance in Bordeaux's history. The structure's striking appearance, featuring a golden leopard weather vane atop, symbolizes the city's historical connection to the English crown during the medieval period.

Beneath its historical grandeur, The Grosse Cloche also bears architectural significance. Its Gothic and Renaissance style features are remarkably well-preserved, offering a glimpse into the craftsmanship of bygone eras. The clock face, added in the 18th century, adds to its charm, making it a popular spot for photographers and history buffs alike.
A visit to The Grosse Cloche isn't just a step back in time; it's an encounter with a living piece of Bordeaux's history. As you stand beneath its massive arches, you're not just in the shadow of a bell tower, but in the presence of centuries of stories, waiting to be discovered in the Pearl of Aquitaine.

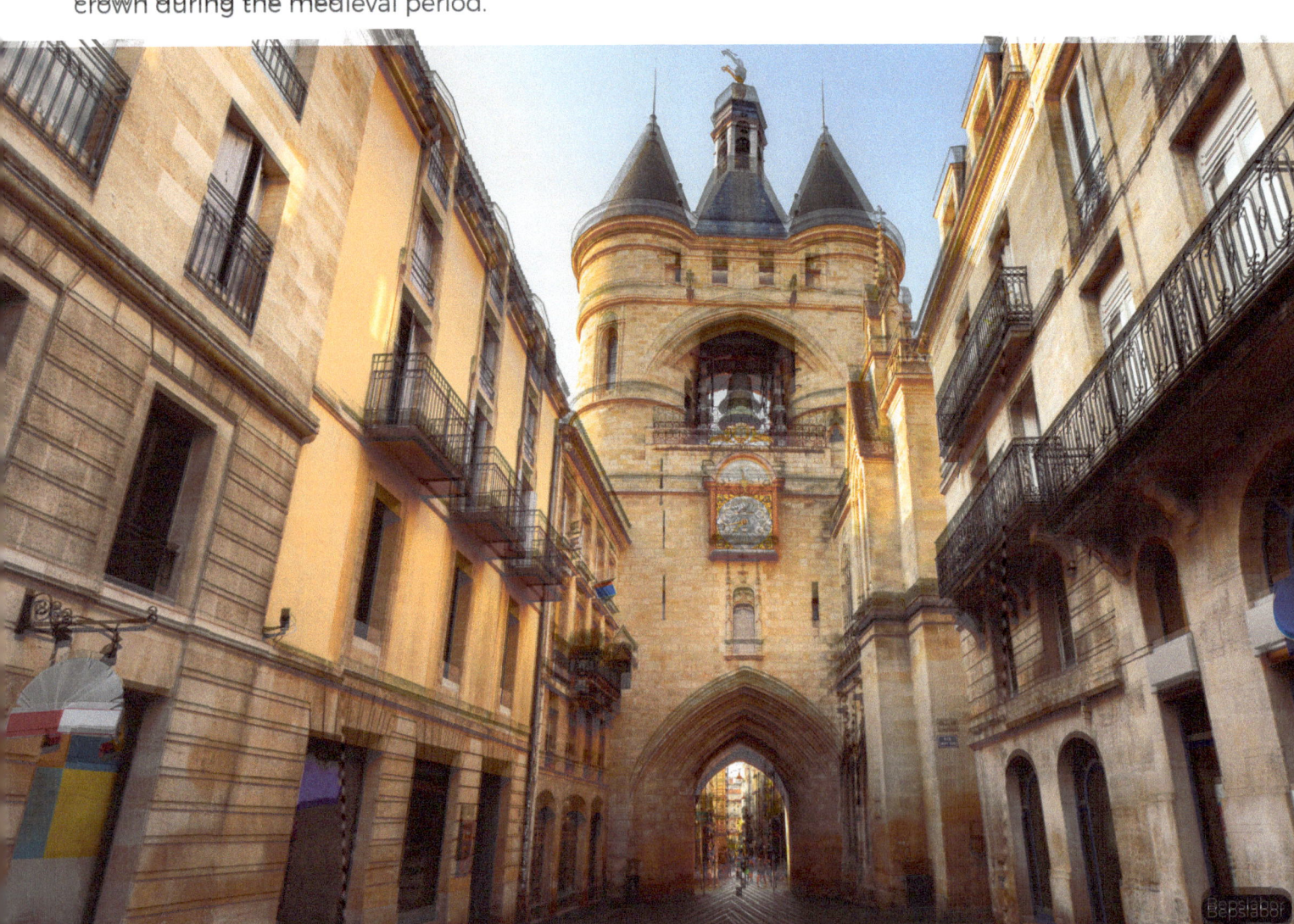

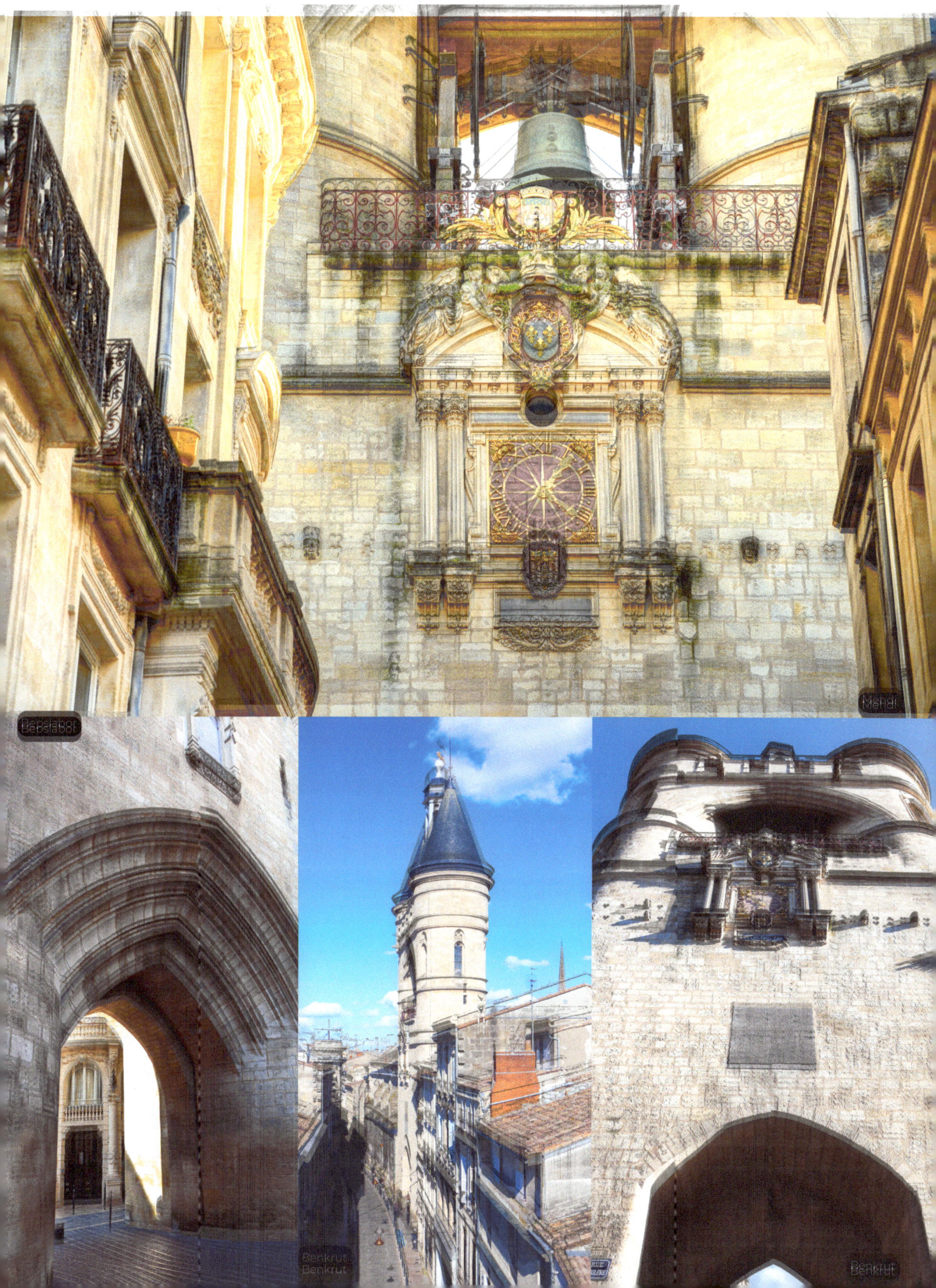

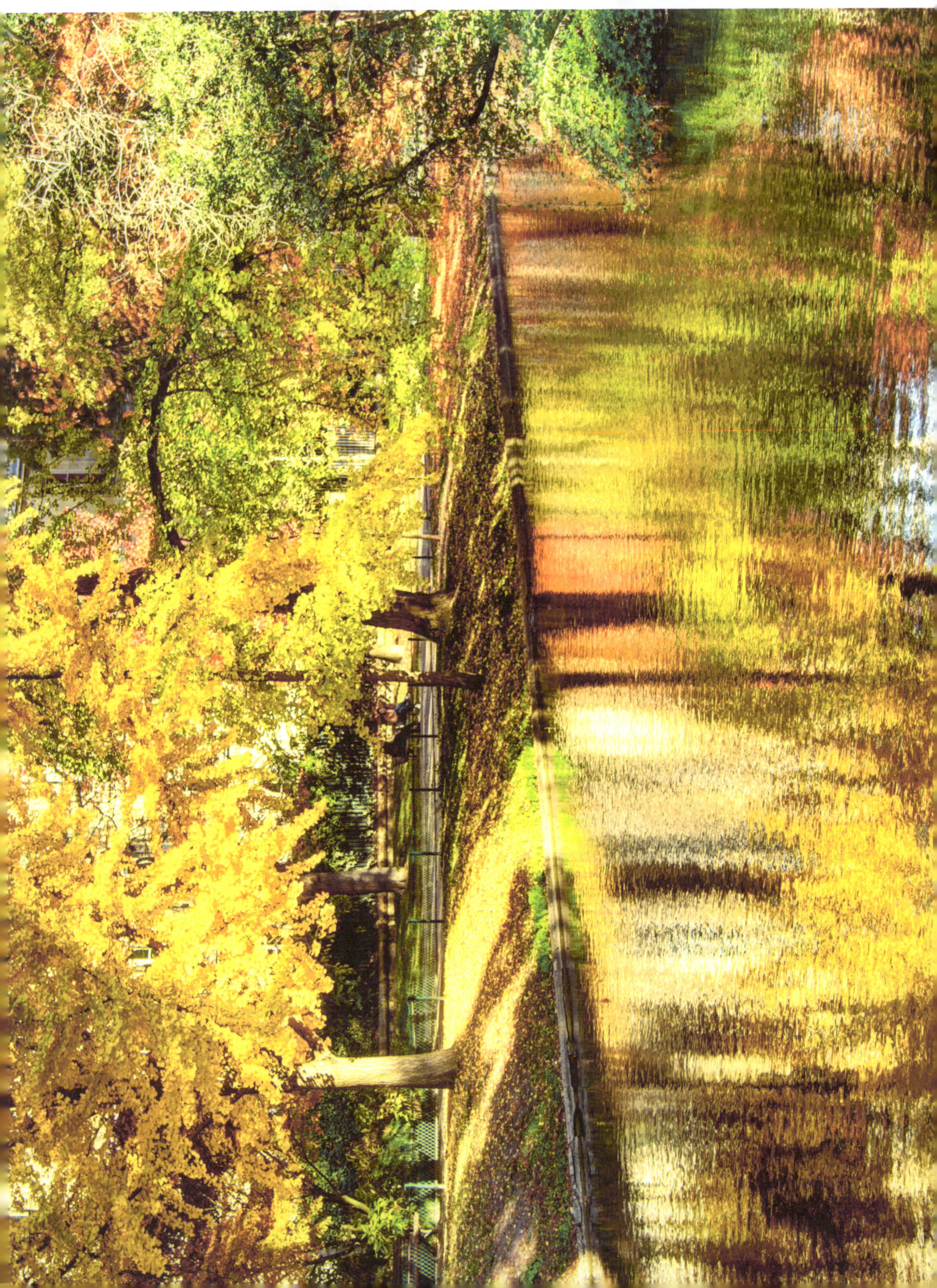

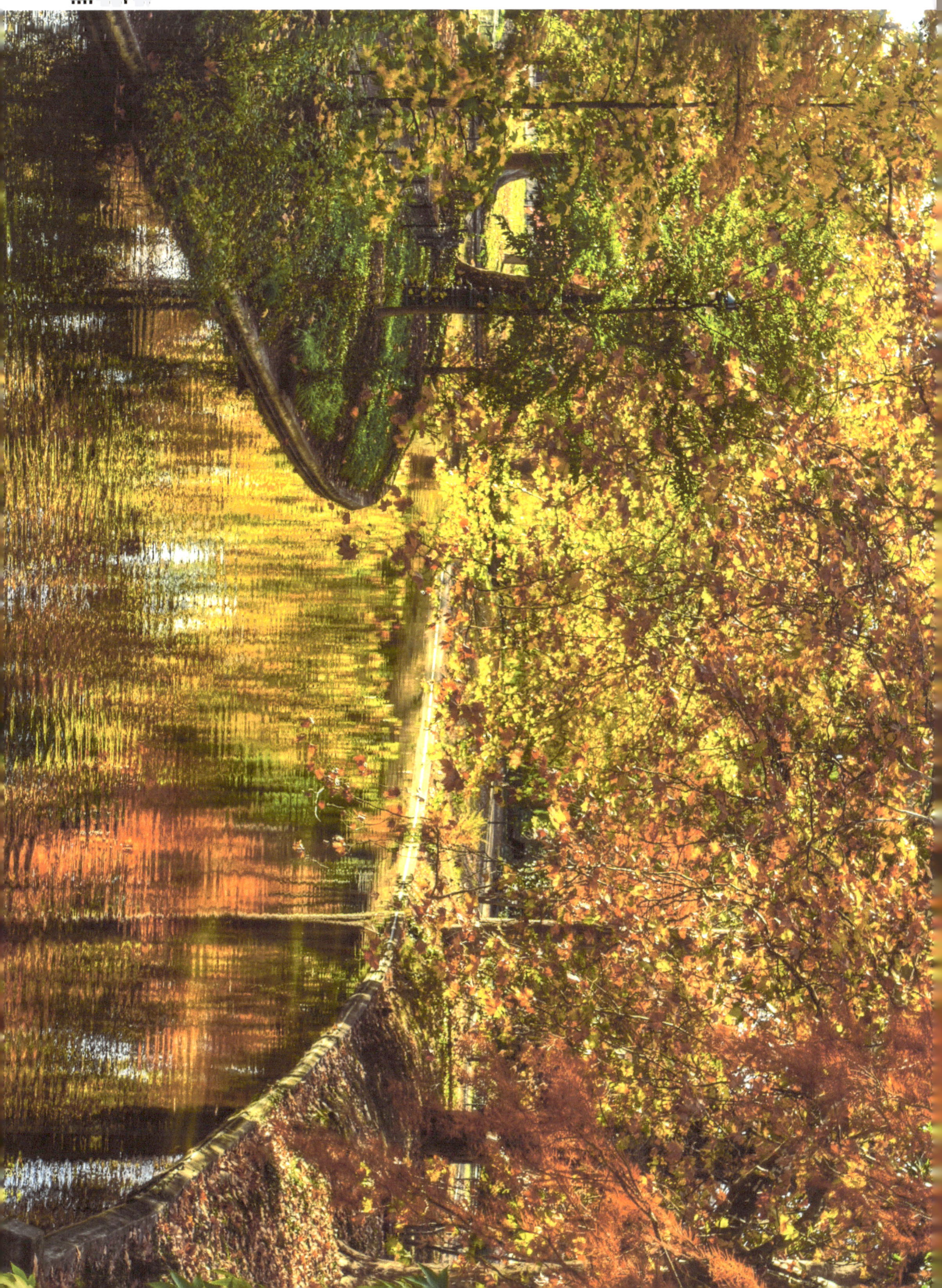

La Cité du Vin

La Cité du Vin, a strikingly modern building rising along the banks of the Garonne River, presents a contemporary twist to Bordeaux's age-old wine narrative. Opened in 2016, this cultural facility reshapes the city's skyline with its bold, curvilinear design, reminiscent of a swirling glass of wine. This architectural marvel is not just a building; it's a sensory journey into the heart of wine culture.

Spanning over 10 floors, La Cité du Vin offers an immersive experience that tantalizes the senses. Its exhibitions are a blend of history, geography, and oenology, providing a global perspective on wine. Interactive displays, multi-sensory experiences, and visually engaging installations guide visitors through the nuances of wine-making traditions from all corners of the world.

The highlight of La Cité du Vin is the Belvedere, located on the eighth floor. Here, visitors are treated to a tasting of world wines, accompanied by a panoramic view of Bordeaux. This experience encapsulates the essence of the city's relationship with wine, offering both a literal and metaphorical taste of its heritage.

La Cité du Vin is more than a museum; it's a celebration of wine as a universal language, connecting people and cultures. It stands as a testament to Bordeaux's legacy as a world wine capital, beckoning connoisseurs and curious visitors alike to explore and indulge in the rich tapestry of wine history.

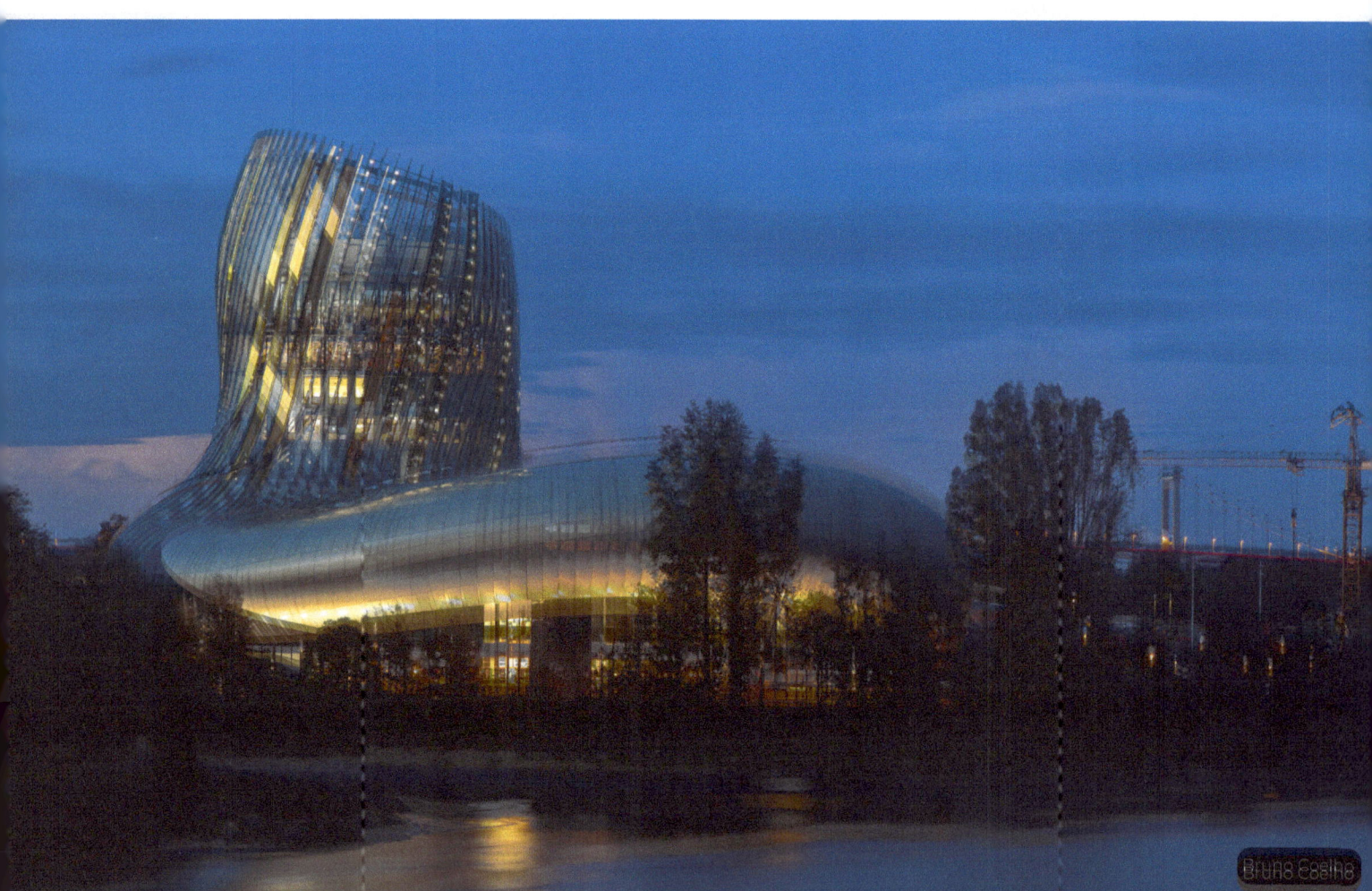

Bruno Coelho

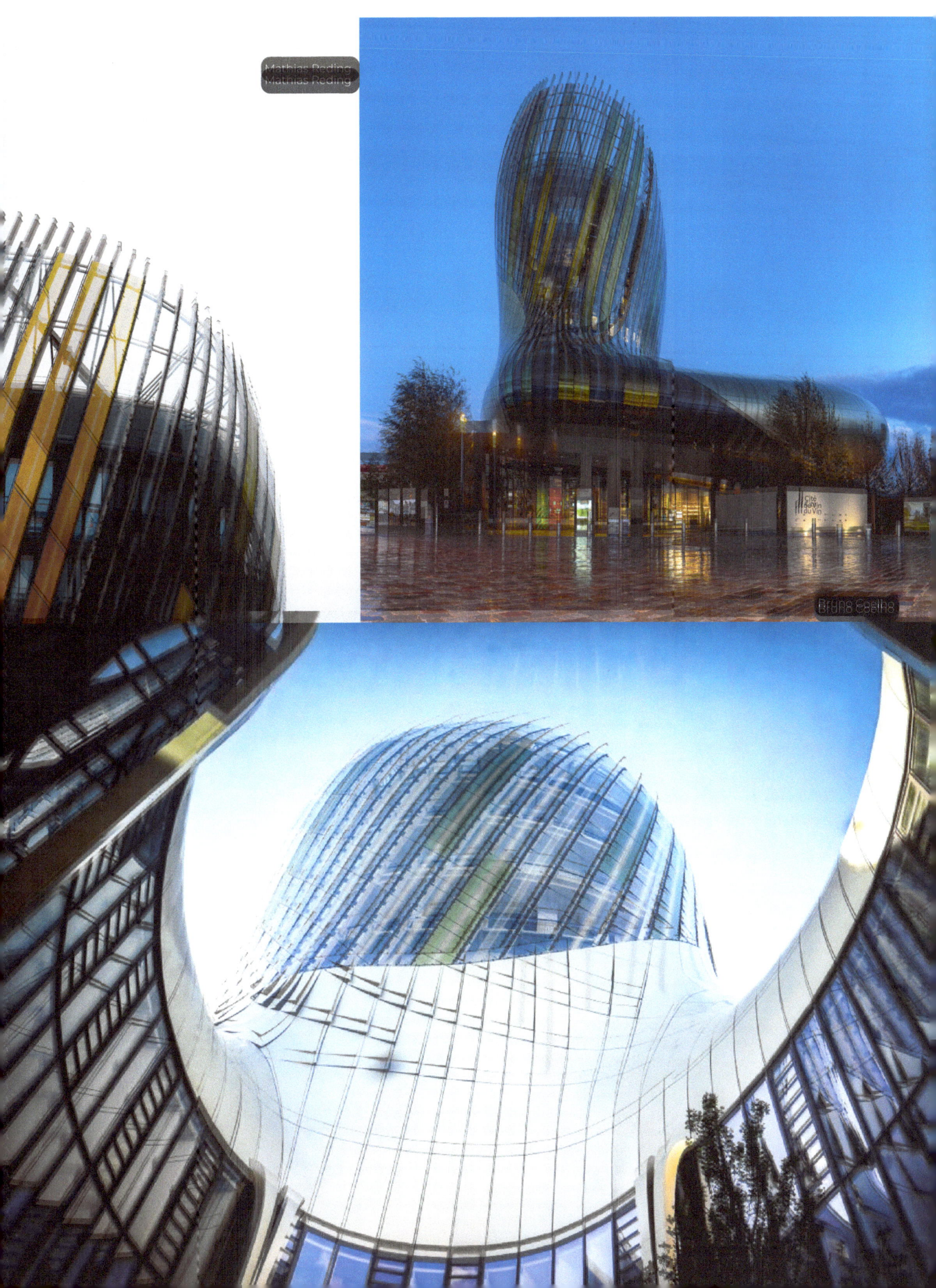

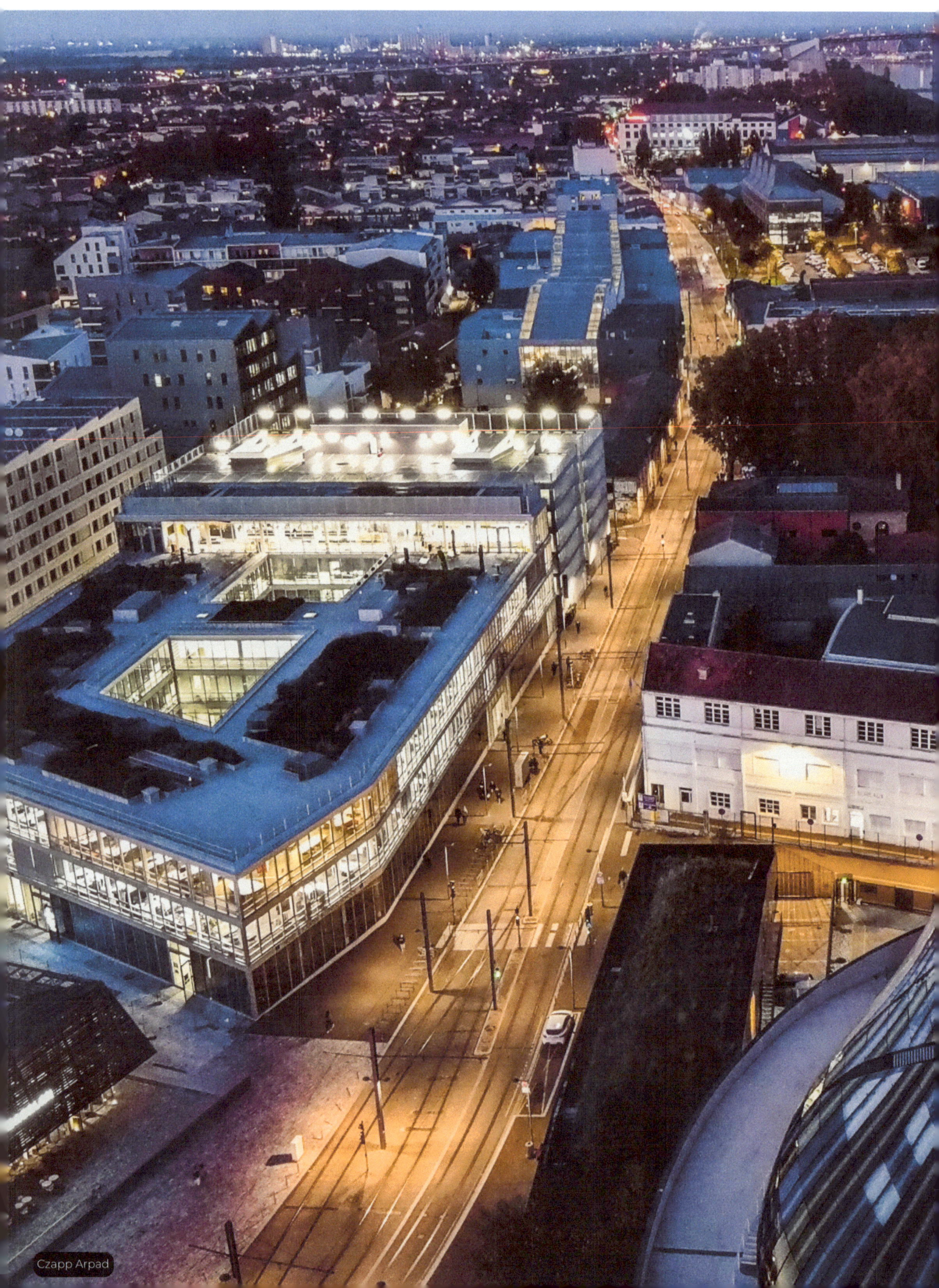
Czapp Árpád

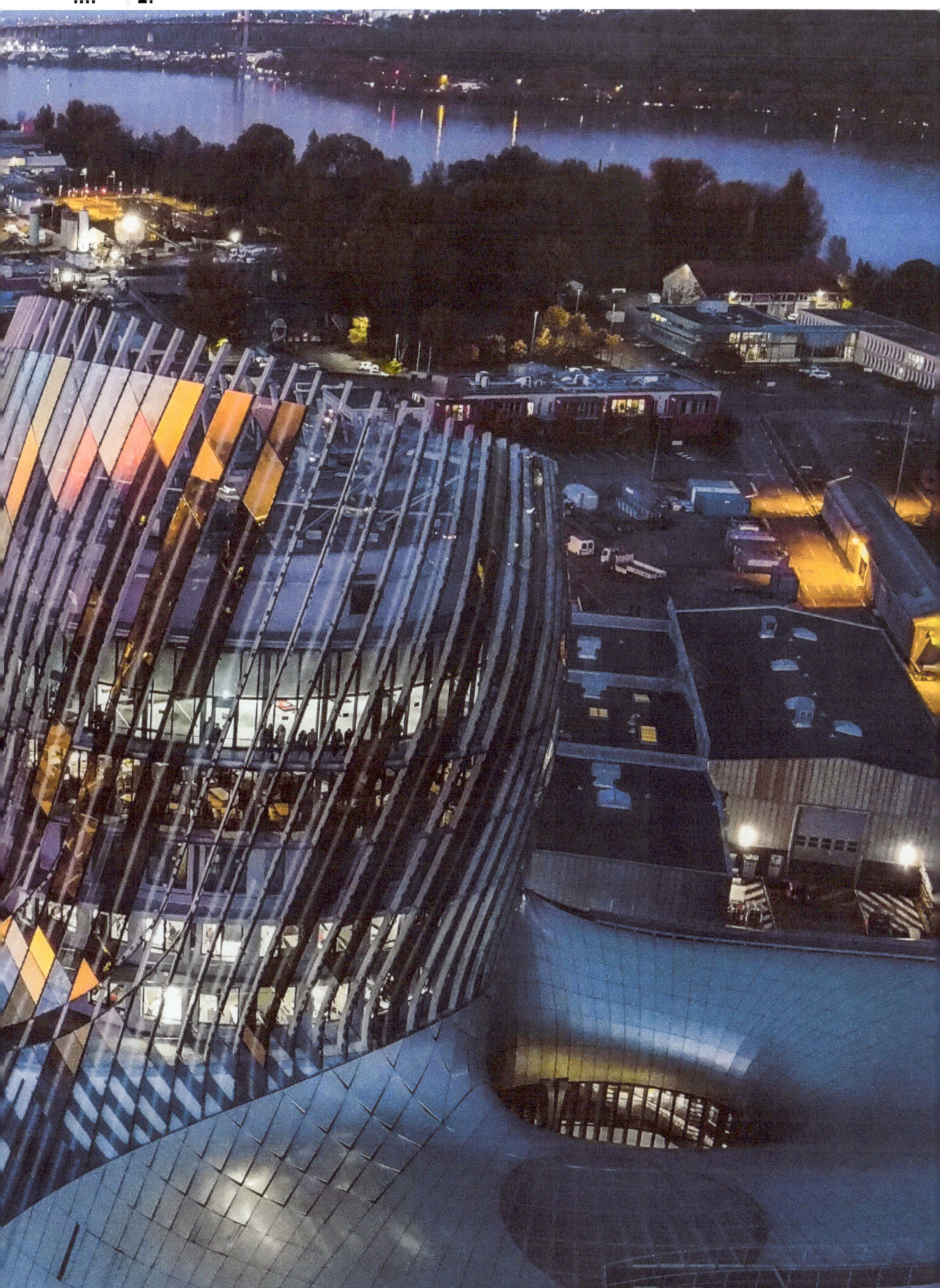

Saint Emilion Vineyard at Sunrise

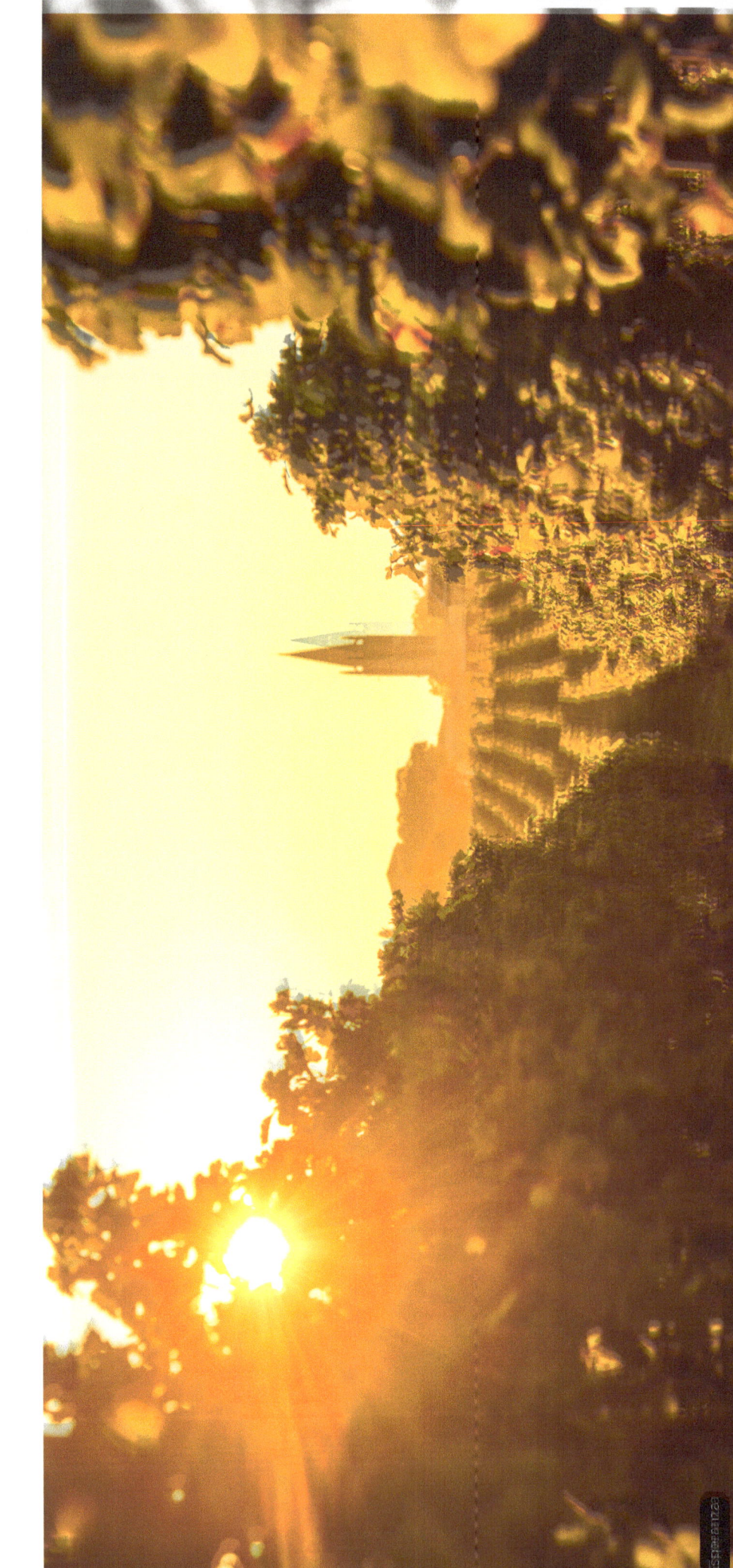

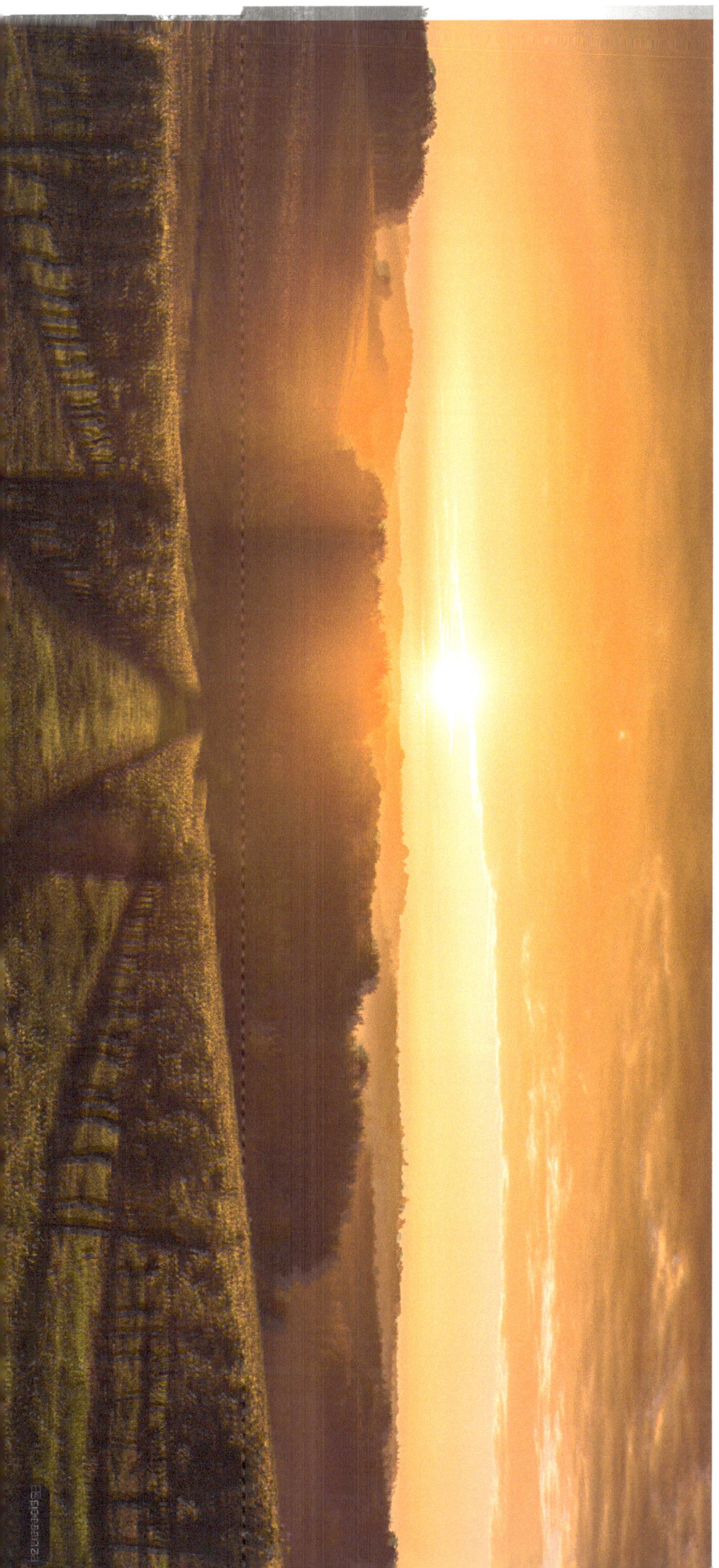

Saint Emilion Vineyard at Sunrise

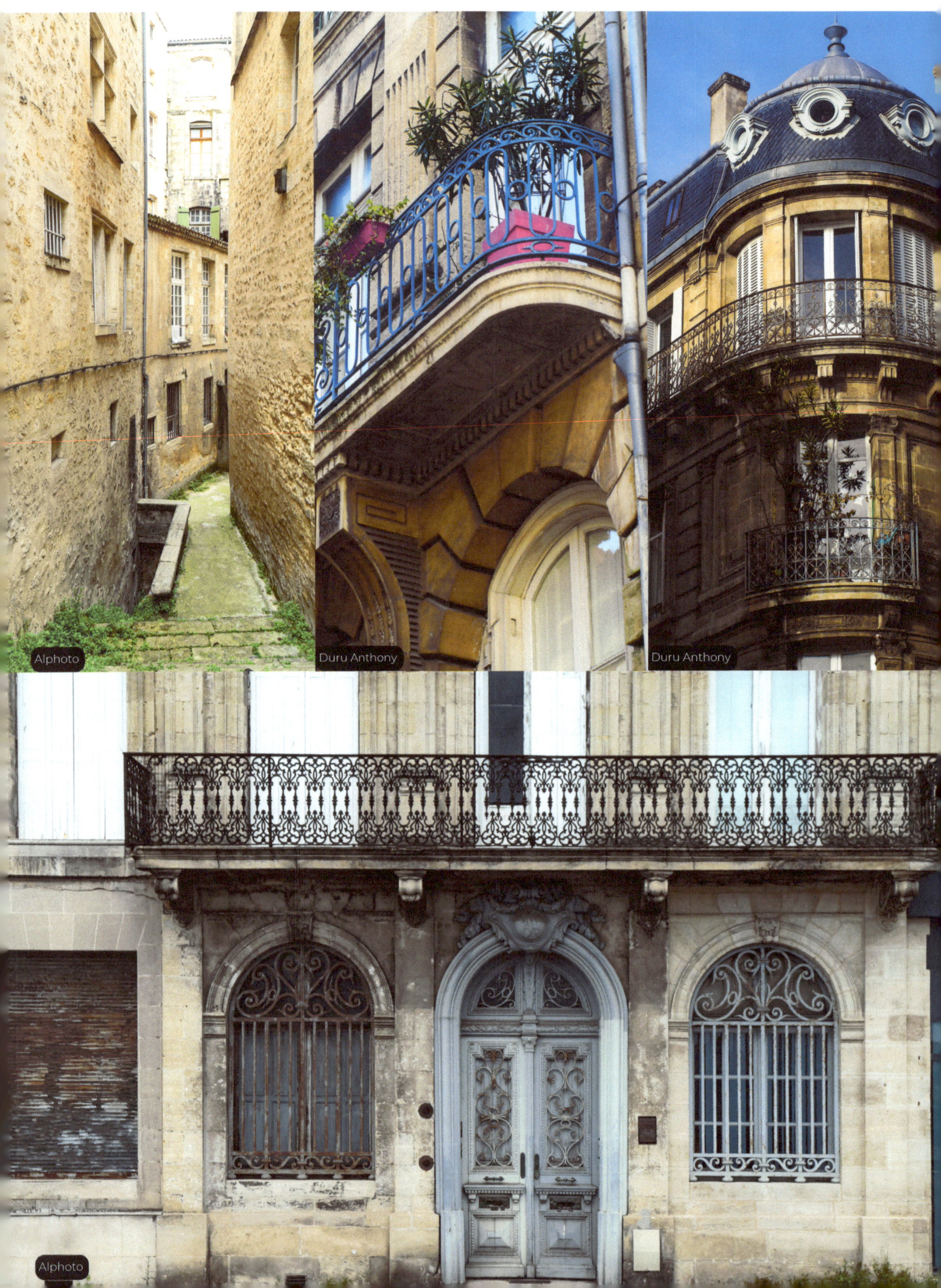

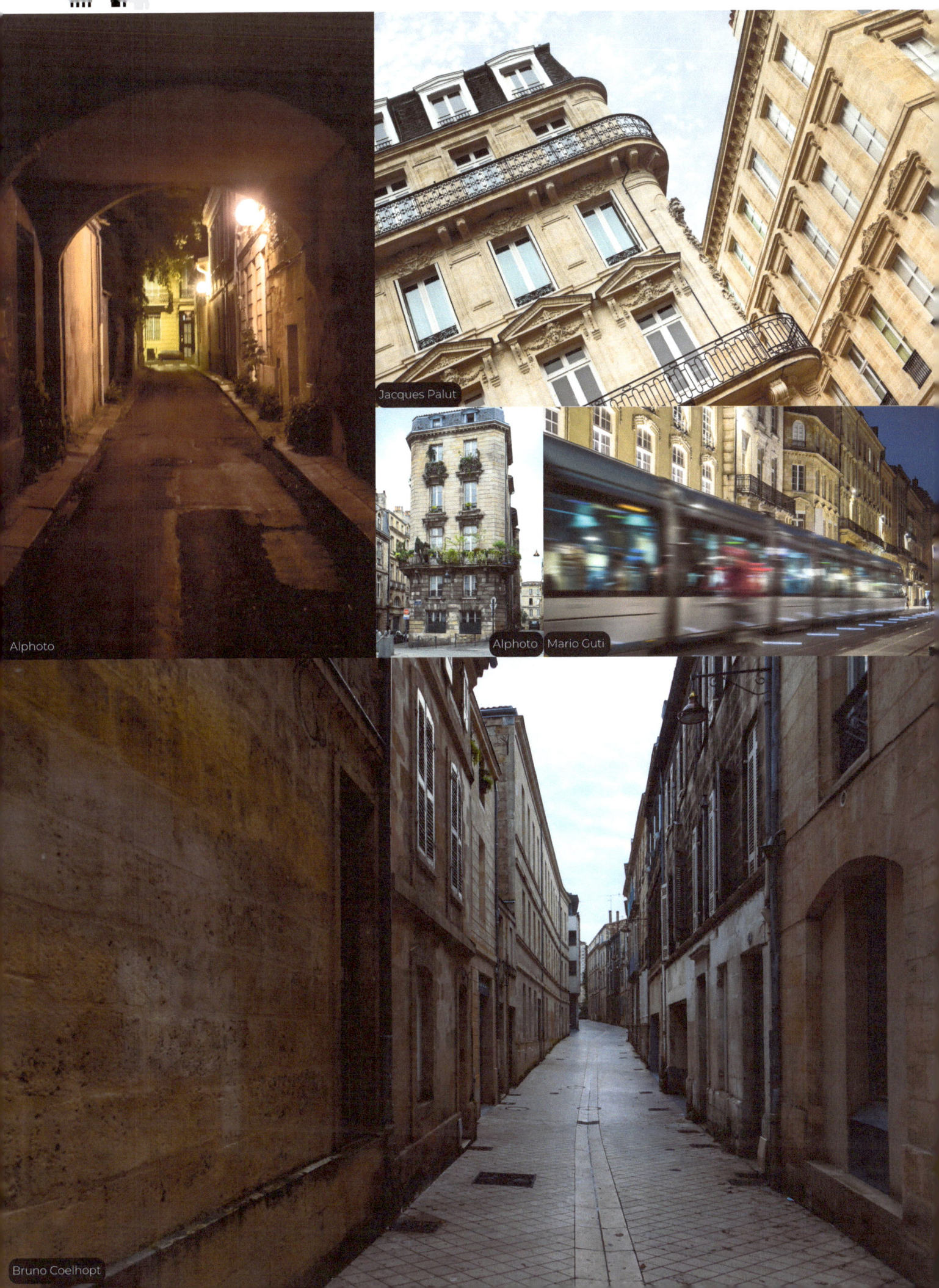

The Grand Théâtre de Bordeaux

The Grand Théâtre de Bordeaux, an architectural masterpiece of the 18th century, stands majestically as a beacon of cultural grandeur in the heart of Bordeaux. Inaugurated in 1780, this neoclassical marvel, designed by architect Victor Louis, is celebrated for its opulent design and historical significance. Its façade, adorned with twelve Corinthian style columns, is topped with statues representing the nine muses and three goddesses, adding to its majestic allure.

Entering the Grand Théâtre, one is transported into an era of extravagant artistry. The grand foyer, with its elaborate frescoes and opulent chandeliers, sets the stage for an experience of timeless elegance. The auditorium, a lavish spectacle of blue, gold, and white, is crowned by a magnificent chandelier. Its horseshoe-shaped layout, renowned for excellent acoustics, has hosted some of the most prestigious operatic and ballet performances.

The Grand Théâtre de Bordeaux is not just a venue for world-class performances; it's a symbol of the city's enduring love affair with the arts. It has witnessed revolutions and restorations, yet remains a steadfast icon of Bordeaux's cultural landscape. A visit here offers more than just a glimpse into the artistic heritage of Bordeaux; it's an encounter with the soul of the city, where every performance is a celebration of artistic brilliance in the Pearl of Aquitaine.

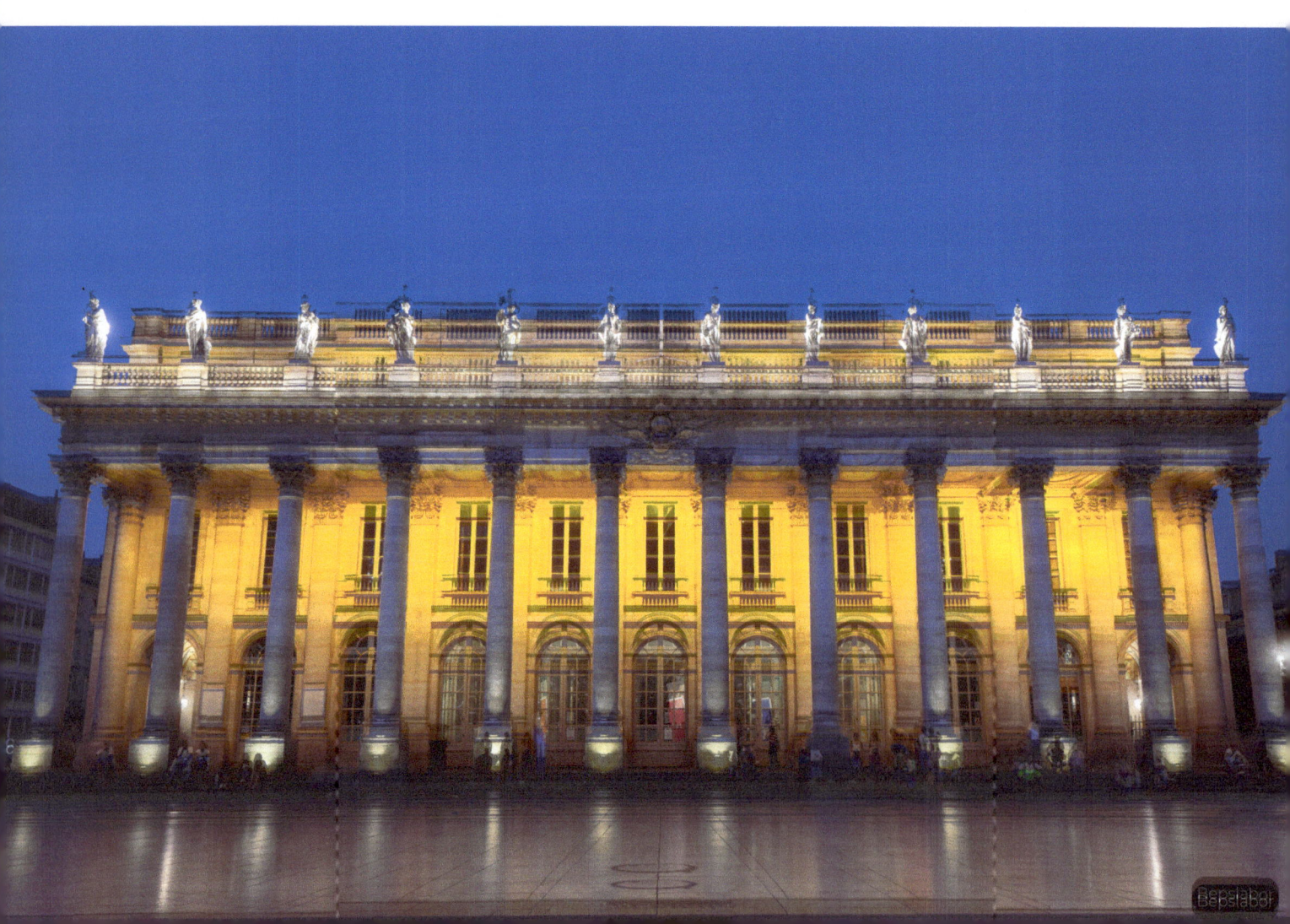

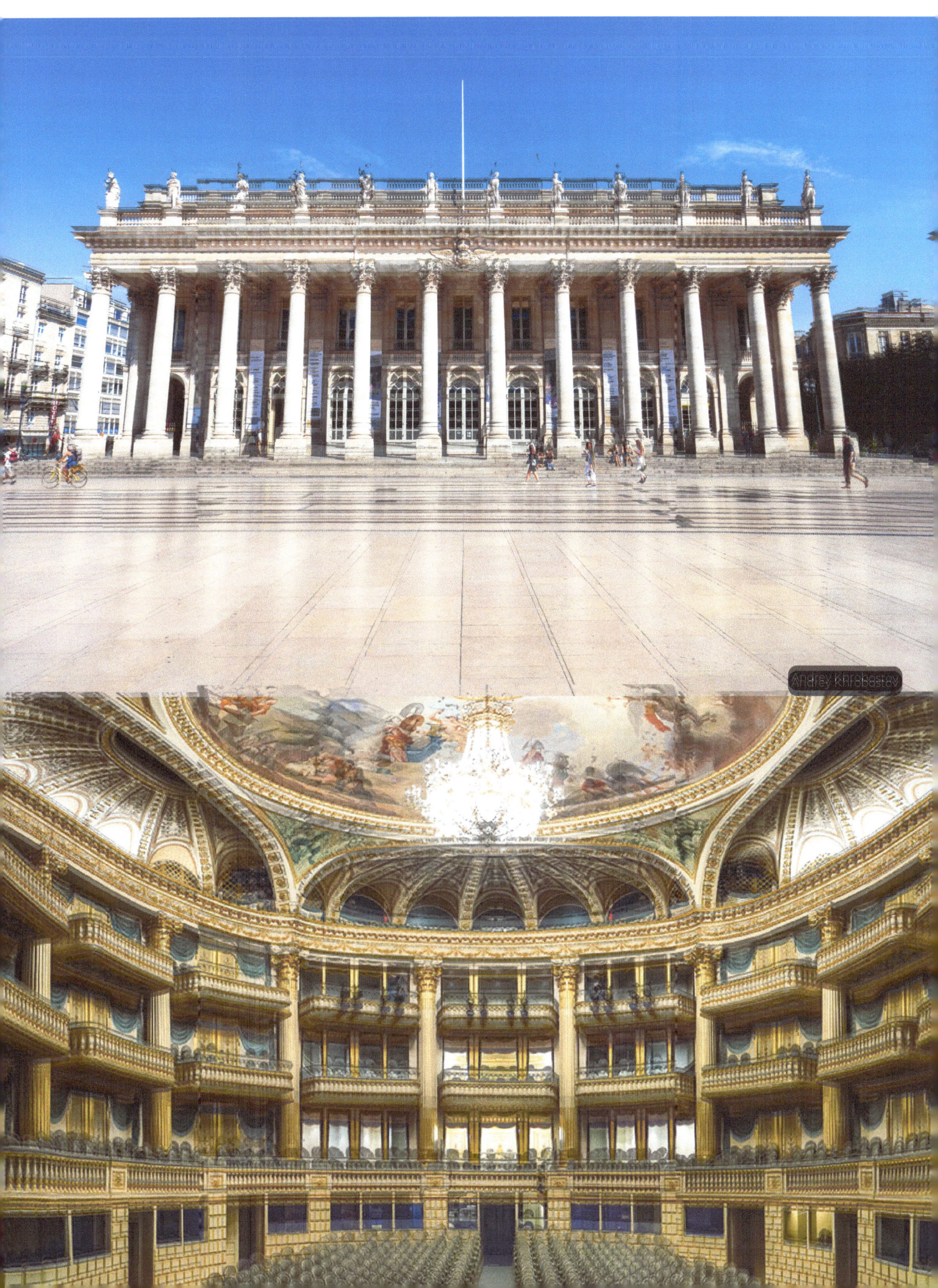

Basilique Saint-Michel

Basilique Saint-Michel, standing in the historic heart of Bordeaux, is an architectural gem that embodies the grandeur of Gothic style. Constructed between the 14th and 16th centuries, this basilica is renowned for its soaring spire, which, at 114 meters, is one of the tallest in France. The spire, separate from the main church, serves as a striking landmark, guiding visitors to this sacred site.

The basilica's exterior is a tapestry of gothic artistry, with intricate stonework and flying buttresses that speak of a bygone era's craftsmanship. The stained glass windows, though restored in the 19th century, retain their medieval essence, casting a serene glow within the church. The interior is equally captivating, with its vast nave, ornate altarpieces, and a remarkable 16th-century century pulpit, exemplifying the intricacy of Gothic wood carving. Basilique Saint-Michel isn't just a place of worship; it's a repository of history and art. The church has a crypt, which, in the past, displayed its collection of mummies, adding an intriguing, albeit macabre, element to its history.

Visitors to Basilique Saint-Michel are treated to more than just architectural beauty. Climbing the 229 steps of the spire offers a breathtaking panoramic view of Bordeaux, providing a unique perspective of the city's blend of historic charm and urban vibrancy. This basilica is a must-visit for those seeking to immerse themselves in the spiritual and historical tapestry of the Pearl of Aquitaine.

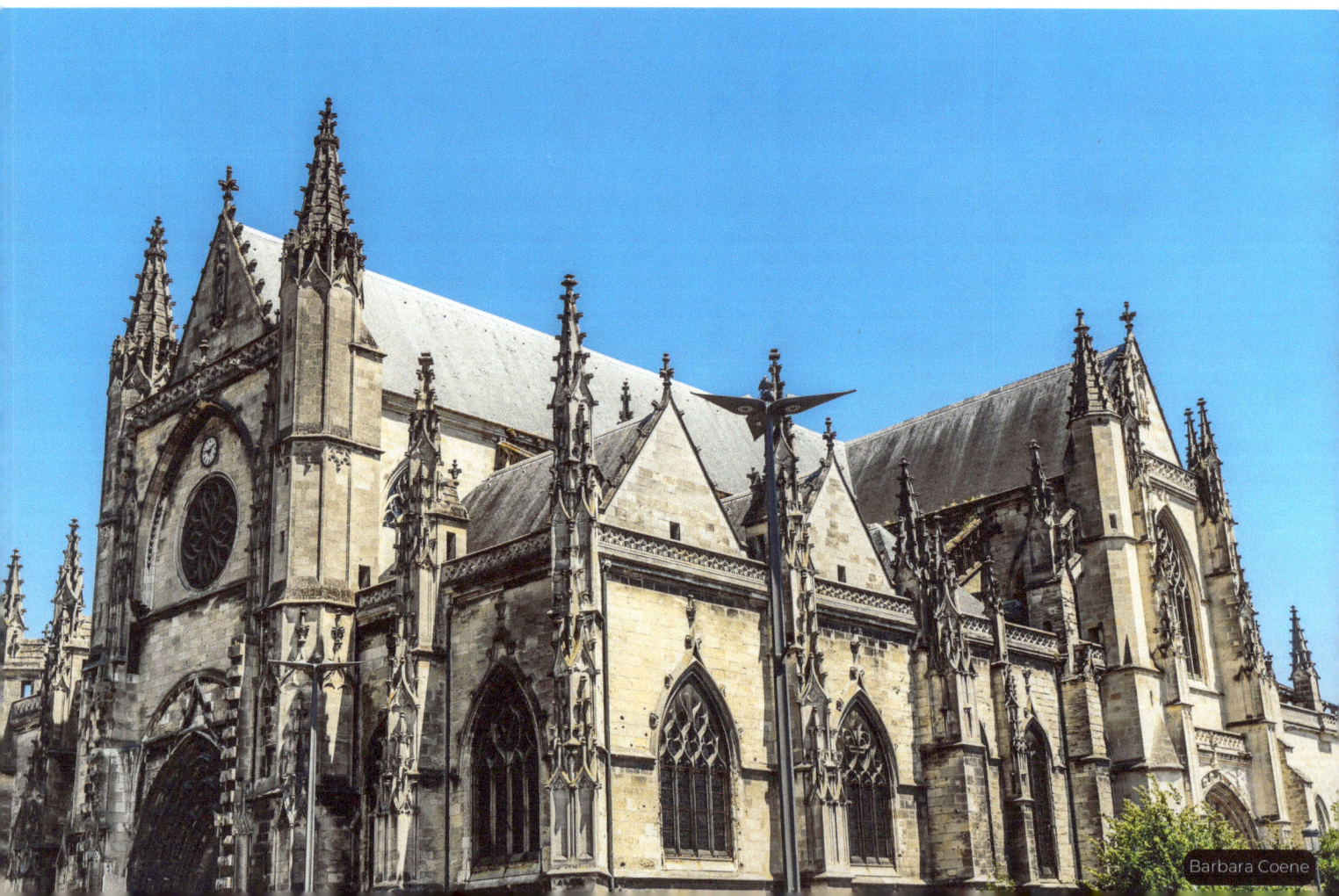
Barbara Coene

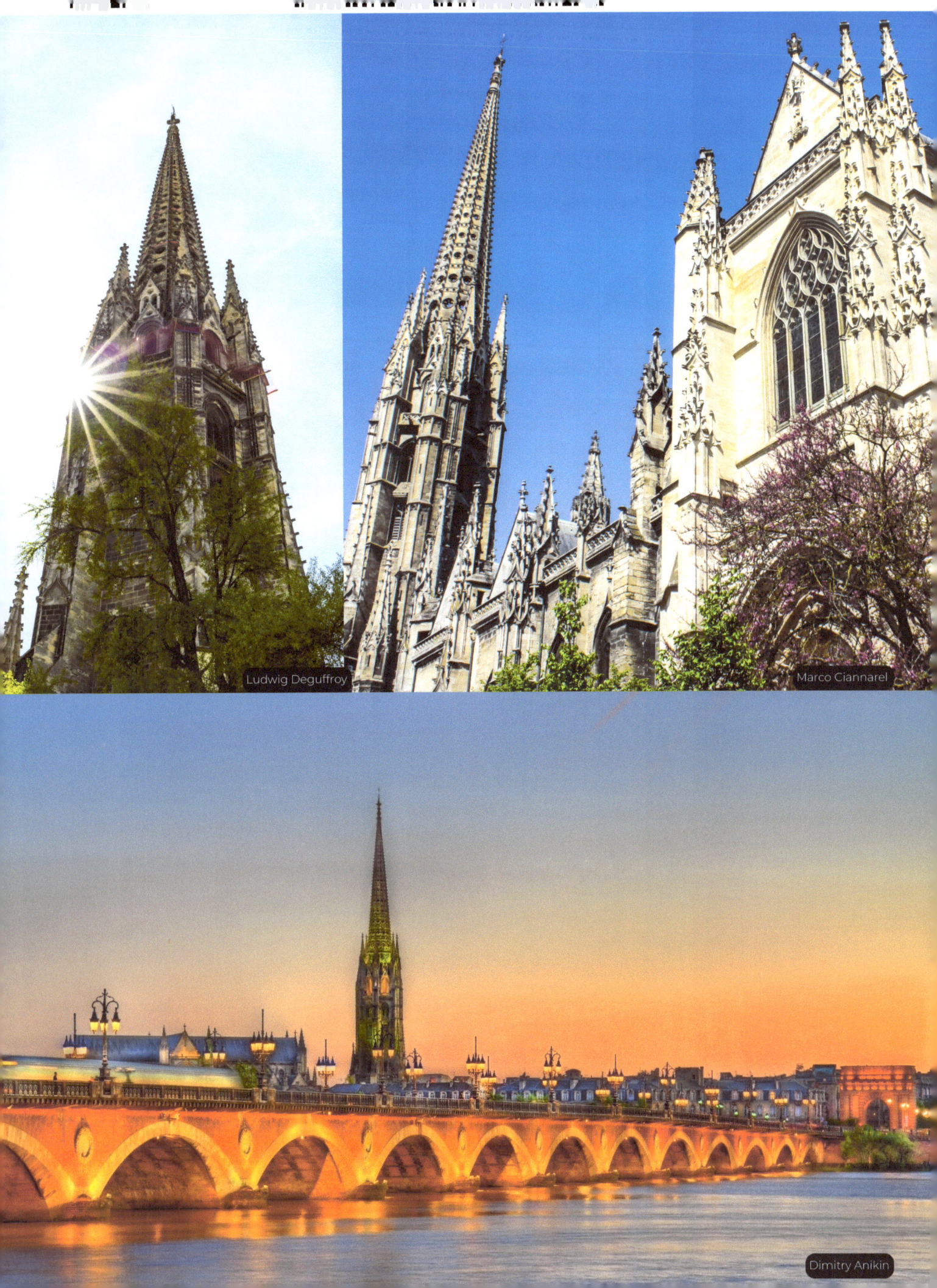

Ludwig Deguffroy

Marco Ciannarel

Dimitry Anikin

Porte de Bourgogne

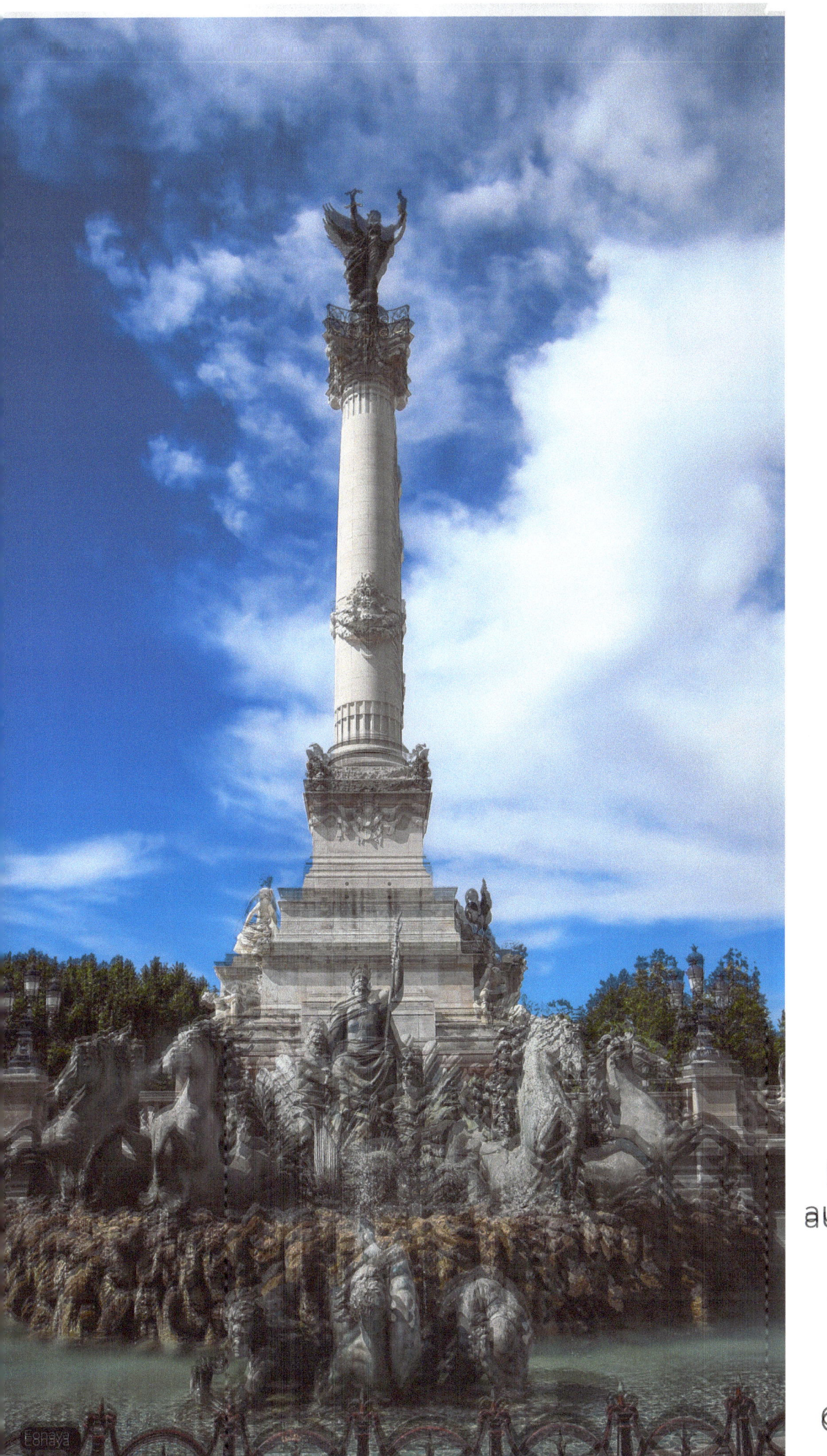

The Monument aux Girondins, located in Bordeaux's expansive Place des Quinconces

Porte Cailhau

Porte Cailhau, a stunning example of Bordeaux's medieval architecture, stands as an imposing gateway to the city's rich past. Erected in 1495 to commemorate King Charles VIII's victory at Fornovo, this 35-meter tall structure was once part of Bordeaux's ancient city walls. Today, it serves as a symbol of the city's historical depth and architectural heritage.

The gate's design is a captivating fusion of defensive and decorative elements. Its Gothic and Renaissance features blend seamlessly, showcasing the transition between two significant architectural eras. The façade facing the river is adorned with sculptures and intricate stonework, featuring a prominent statue of Charles VIII, while the city-facing side retains a more robust, fortress-like appearance.

Visitors entering through Porte Cailhau are immediately struck by the contrast between the medieval structure and the bustling urban life of Bordeaux. Inside, a small museum provides insights into the gate's history and offers a journey through the architectural evolution of the city. Climbing to the top, one is rewarded with panoramic views of the Garonne River and the surrounding cityscape, a vista that connects the past with the present.

Porte Cailhau is more than just a historical monument; it's a tangible connection to the stories and legends that have shaped Bordeaux. As a gateway to the city's heart, it invites visitors to step back in time and experience the enduring legacy of the Pearl of Aquitaine.

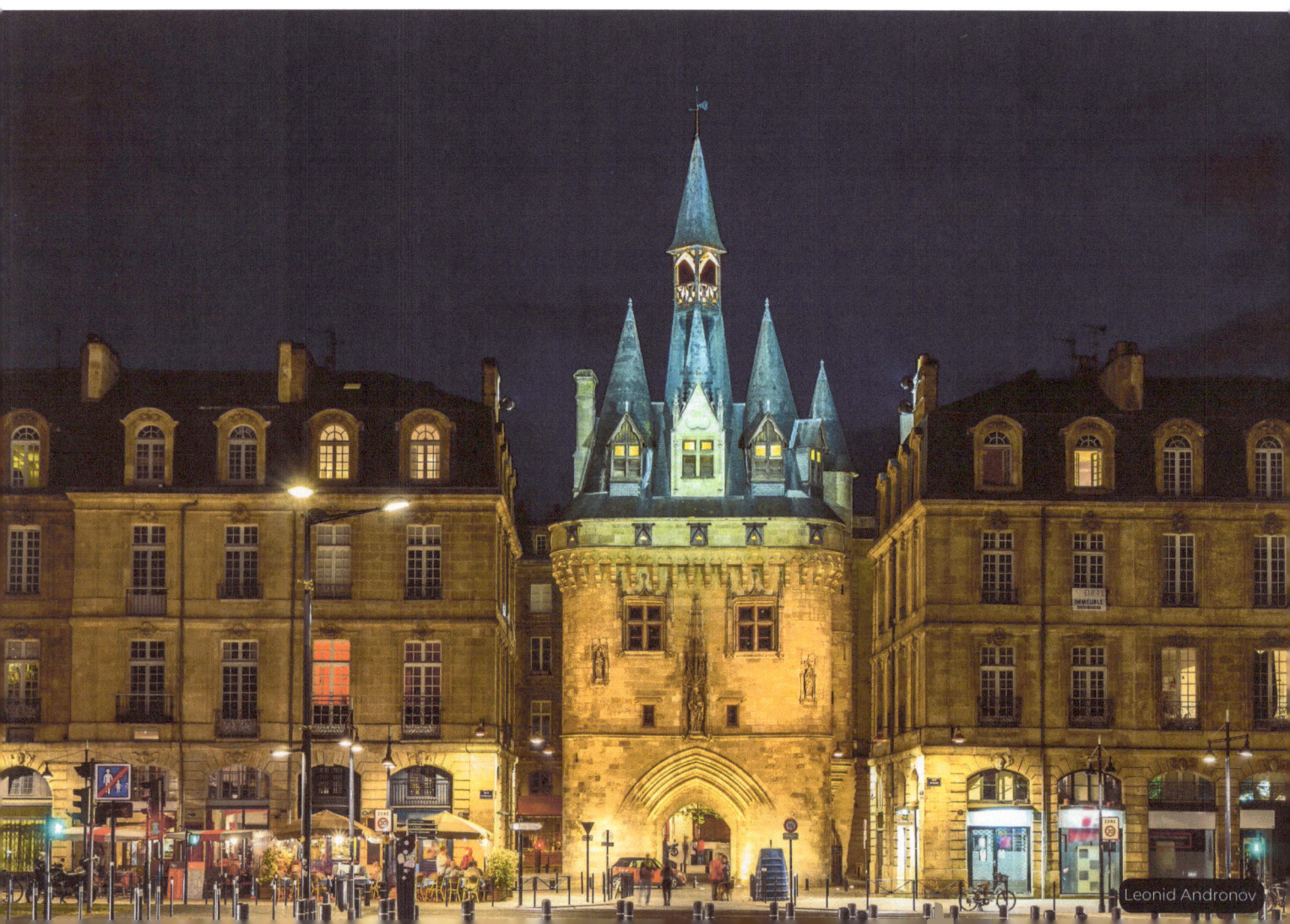

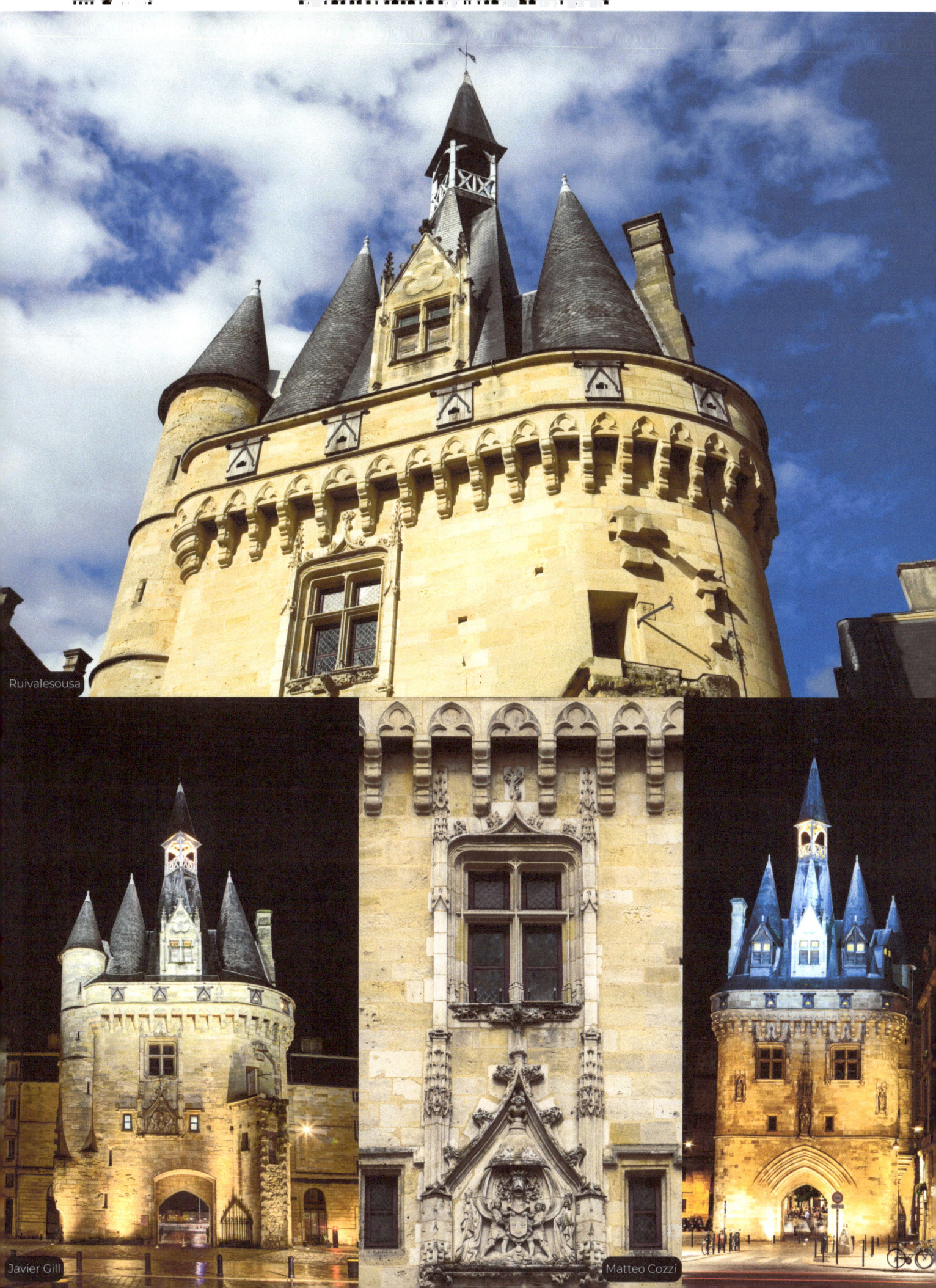

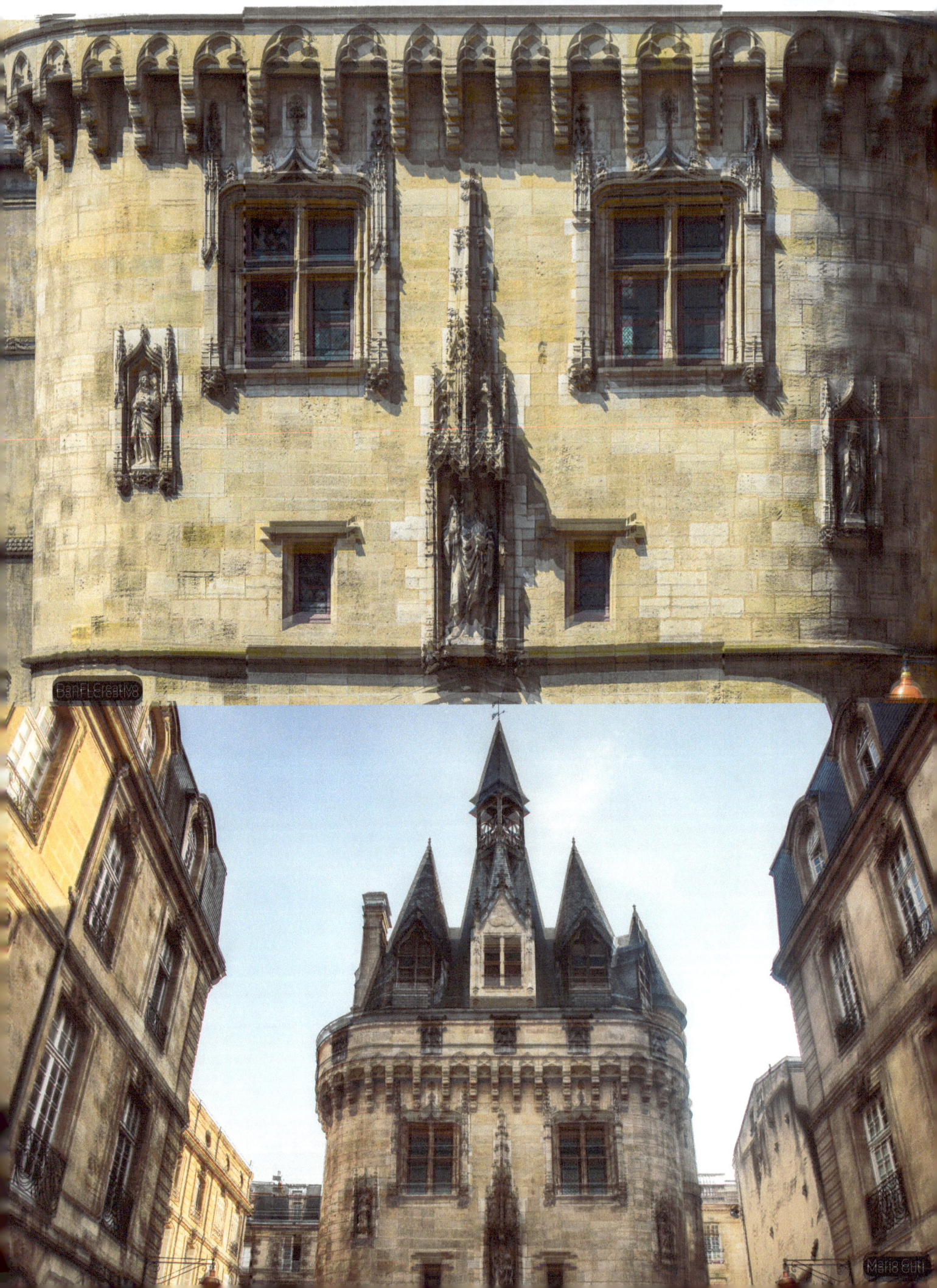

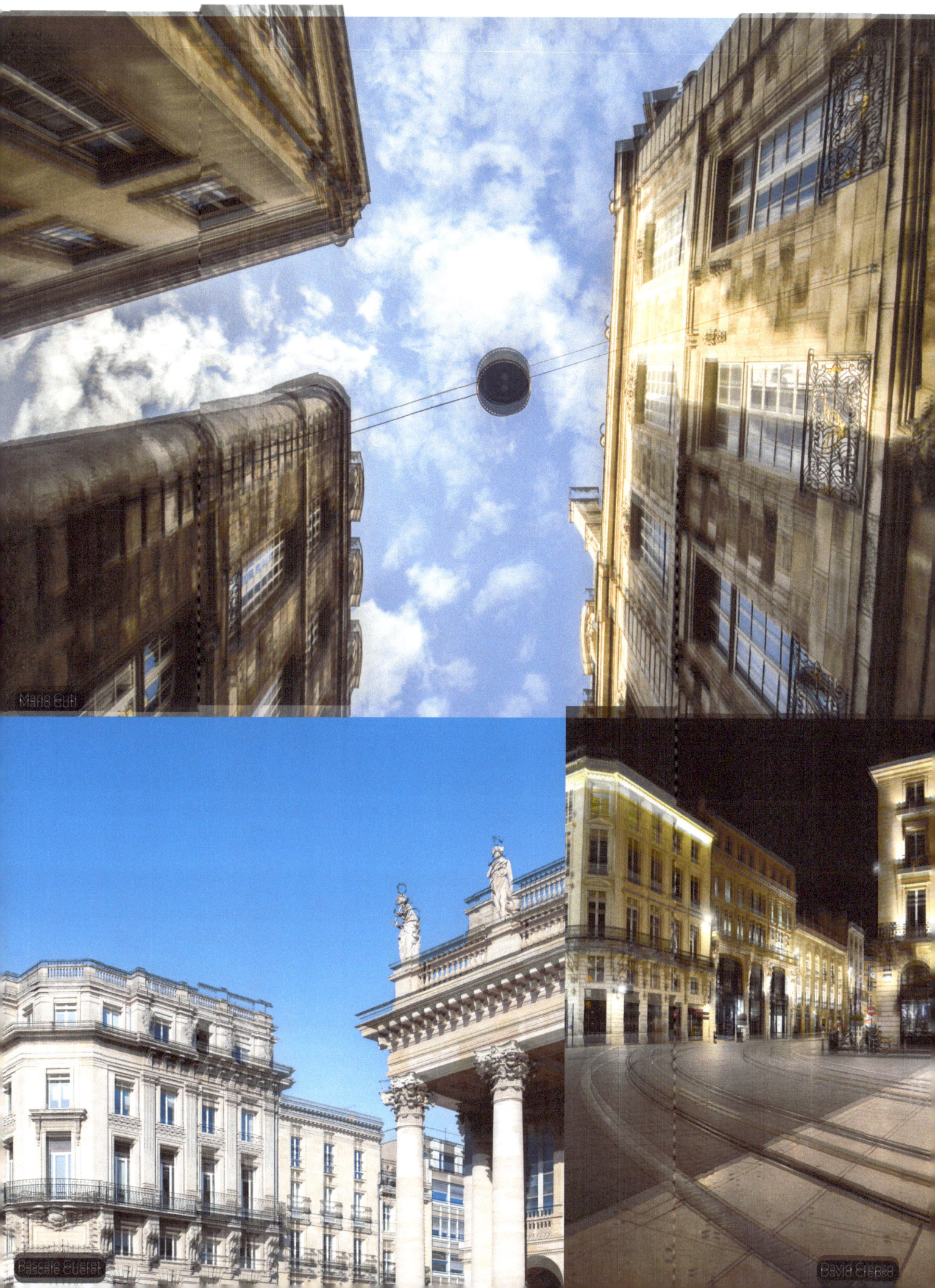

"Discovering Bordeaux - The Pearl of Aquitaine Pictorial" has offered a visual journey through the city's stunning landmarks, from the gothic splendor of its cathedrals to the modern allure of La Cité du Vin. Each page has been a testament to Bordeaux's rich history and vibrant culture. For those inspired to delve deeper into this enchanting city, "UNVEILING BORDEAUX - Your Travel Guide to The Pearl of Aquitaine" is your essential companion. This comprehensive guide invites you to explore hidden gems and immerse yourself in the local lifestyle, uncovering new layers of beauty and fascination in Bordeaux's timeless charm. Join us in uncovering the heart of the Pearl of Aquitaine

UNVEILING BORDEAUX

Your Travel Guide to The Pearl of Aquitaine

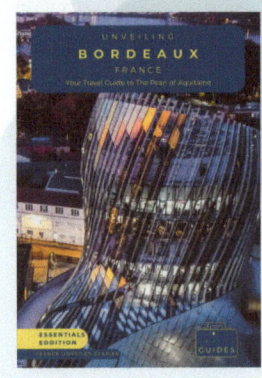

CHECK OUT THE FRANCE UNVEILED TRAVEL GUIDES SERIES

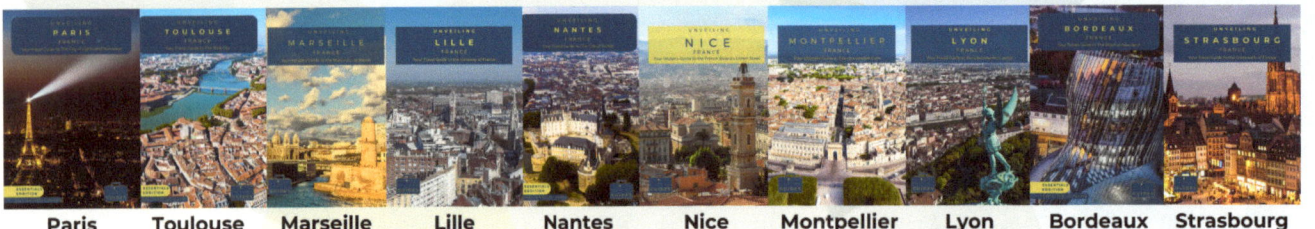

Paris | Toulouse | Marseille | Lille | Nantes | Nice | Montpellier | Lyon | Bordeaux | Strasbourg

CHECK OUT THE ITALY UNCOVERED TRAVEL GUIDES SERIES

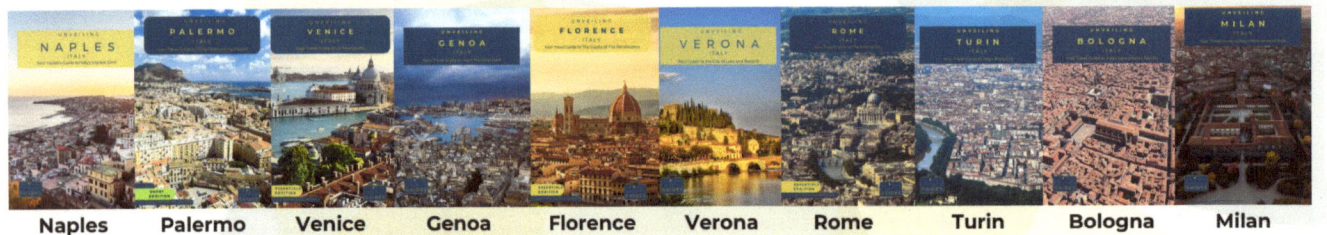

Naples | Palermo | Venice | Genoa | Florence | Verona | Rome | Turin | Bologna | Milan

CHECK OUT THE SPAIN UNVEILED TRAVEL GUIDES SERIES

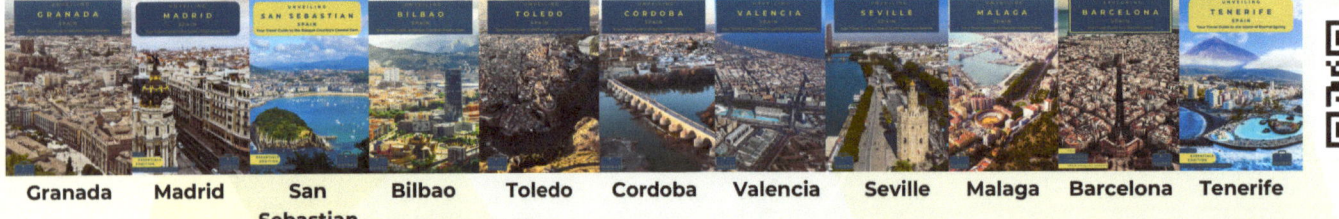

Granada | Madrid | San Sebastian | Bilbao | Toledo | Cordoba | Valencia | Seville | Malaga | Barcelona | Tenerife

Join our Tailored Travel Guides Network for more benefits by accessing this link:
https://mailchi.mp/d151cba349e8/ttgnetwork
Or by scanning the QR code

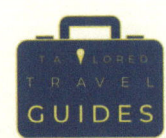

Discover your journey!

www.ingramcontent.com/pod-product-compliance
Lightning Source LLC
Chambersburg PA
CBHW051932210526
45473CB00006B/2227